The
CLEAR
Method

The
CLEAR
Method

THE EASY WAY TO
DECLUTTER YOUR CHAOS
AND FIND YOUR SPARKLE

Carolyn Creel

THE UNBOUND PRESS

ISBN 978-1-913590-91-8 Paperback

ISBN 978-1-913590-92-5 Ebook

The Unbound Press
www.theunboundpress.com

Hey unbound one!

Welcome to this magical book brought to you by The Unbound Press.

At The Unbound Press we believe that when women write freely from the fullest expression of who they are, it can't help but activate a feeling of deep connection and transformation in others. When we come together, we become more and we're changing the world, one book at a time!

This book has been carefully crafted by both the author and publisher with the intention of inspiring you to move ever more deeply into who you truly are.

We hope that this book helps you to connect with your Unbound Self and that you feel called to pass it on to others who want to live a more fully expressed life.

With much love,

Nicola Humber

Founder of The Unbound Press

www.theunboundpress.com

"The CLEAR Method is for Everyone.
Practically, it declutters the chaos of life
And Energetically it helps you to see more clearly."

Carolyn Creel

CONTENTS

Welcome

"Above all, I wish to see."
— Donna Goddard, Circles of Separation

Welcome to The CLEAR Method.

This little book is the equivalent of you and me having a cup of good ol' PG tips tea, and sitting down for a chat about changing your space, your energy, and your life.

Now, a few things to get us started, lovely; you will find that I say things as they are.

I am an old bird, and a Yorkshire old bird, at that.

So, any notions of floaty kaftans, wind chimes, and waft – forget it.

I am 'woo,' yes, absolutely – I don't think you can call yourself a clairvoyant cleaner, talk to Spirit and not be woo, can you? But, I am definitely one woo, not two.

I have my feet on the earth, and you'll find I am a straight-talking, no fluff, Northern business woman who happens to be an expert in cleaning; cleaning offices in one business, and cleaning energy fields in another.

More on that later in the book.

For now, let's just celebrate that you are here with me.

Maybe your life feels too overwhelming.

Maybe you are going through some big shifts.

Maybe you want to connect to your purpose, to your intuition, or you are looking for some guidance in life.

This book is like having me in your corner, helping you to make the smallest changes that make all the difference. And I am cheering you on all the way.

So, whatever brought you here, I am so glad to be with you as we start this journey together, taking the first step to explore what The CLEAR Method might bring to your life.

Love, Carolyn x

How to Use this Book

This book is intended to be something you can dip into, to use as you need, and come back to again and again, because, let's face it, energy and spaces all need refreshing regularly.

I want you to feel better inside, enjoy a better life than you had before, and leave feeling clearer.

Ever found yourself stuck? Unsure of what to do next; and then you have a major blitz of your kitchen cupboards, just because... and I'm betting after that, you feel so much better about whatever it was keeping you stuck?

This is the CLEAR method in all its glory. I mean there is a reason why we spring clean and welcome in the new season.

CLEARing isn't new. It's something that used to be handed down through the generations, and in the age of 'stuff' and 'clutter' it's easy to forget.

I will talk a little about the woo stuff too. In fact did you know that Clairvoyant means 'seeing clearly'… more on that later!

I would love to share with you the methods I use regularly, which I have in turn passed down to my own daughter and those who come to me for guidance.

I've written the book based on each letter – and then segmented those letters based on the big things in life where we often need guidance and clarity of thought.

So you can flick to the place you need guidance on; or you can follow it to the literal letter!

What I do want to share before you dive in, is that sometimes clearing our spaces can be overwhelming, which is why so many of us don't do it, especially if we are doing it because of a major life event and we feel pushed into it, but it really doesn't have to be.

My guidance is to take it slowly, keep it simple and only do it when you are in 'the flow.'

I've also included in each section short quizzes and self-assessments which may help you get into the CLEAR zone.

There is no 'perfect' timeline to achieve anything, when it comes to CLEARing. Your own timeline is perfect. Each time you go through this book, it might be different – and that's perfect too.

You'll also come to realise that sections C and L go very much hand in hand; it is hard to Clear, when you can't Let Go.

So go at your pace, take small actions, knowing it's still progress. But most of all be gentle with yourself and most importantly have fun!

My Story

How I went from cleaning offices
to helping people declutter their lives

Well, since we are going to be hanging out together while you CLEAR, let's get acquainted, shall we?

My name is Carolyn. I am a Mum, a brand new, super proud Grandma, an entrepreneur, dog lover, and clairvoyant clearer.

My story is all about cleaning, in one way or another.

It's also about resilience, moving through tough times, and creating your own path, which we will be exploring together through these pages, as my story intertwines with yours.

As a kid, I grew up in a small market town in North Yorkshire. I was the youngest of two daughters of a self-employed butcher; my Grandfather and Uncle were also butchers, so clearly it was a family thing.

I was very aware of Spirit from a young age.

I could always feel energy, too; things like a drop in temperature, swirling colours surrounding people, other people's emotions, and even shadows were normal for me to see and be aware of.

My mother told me that I had invisible friends, and people I used to talk to but she could never see.

In fact, after my Grandfather passed away, he came to visit me. I was about 15 at the time, and tucked up in bed. He appeared at the end of my bed and told me he knew I could see him, and could I tell the family he was happy and at peace.

I passed the message on, and I know my family felt comforted by it.

Being quite honest, as a child I thought everyone had the same ability as me, so I didn't really make a thing of it.

It wasn't just Spirit I could feel. I was also very good at sizing people up, reading them, and tapping into energy and emotions. For example, I could absolutely *never* understand why people would want to write in to Jim'll Fix It! I could absolutely feel the creepy, dark energy surrounding him and wanted nothing to do with it.

As I was growing up, we lived behind a cemetery – and let me tell you, it used to spook me out! After I was visited by a particularly scary spirit, I asked the spirits to not show themselves any more, and so for a while I stopped seeing them.

Asking Spirit to work with you where you are right now

I am a clairvoyant and psychic, but I definitely do NOT like to see manifestations and apparitions. There is no 'I see dead people' twist here. Heck no.

Years ago, I asked Spirit to not show me spirits like that, after one particularly jolting experience.

I was straightening my hair in front of the mirror one morning – the kind of moment where I might often get inspiration, messages, thoughts, or guidance. If you get ideas that strike while you are in the shower or washing up, pottering about the house, you will know exactly what I mean.

I saw something in the corner of my vision, and when I turned to look, there was a massive bloke, an enormous guy. Just sitting in the corner of the room.

I totally freaked out, shut my eyes, and said, "No, no! Don't show me spirits like that. Please put them in my mind's eyes, my third eye, like a vision – but do not put them at the side of me so I see them in physical form." I really am a scaredy cat when it comes to things like that. Spirits have never appeared to me that way since, and I am much, much happier seeing them as visions or sensing them.

As we do this work and connect to intuition, to your higher self, remember that we still have free will. We can ask Spirit at any time to dial it down a bit for us, to make it manageable, and they will respect it.

As I grew older, I chose to ignore the feelings, the signs from Spirit, and this intuitive part of me, and just got on with life.

I got married, I had a daughter, and looked for a 'proper job,' which led to working for various cleaning companies over the years.

Twenty years ago, and a single mother by then, I decided to set up my own company with a colleague.

We started with nothing, and built the business from the ground up.

It was hard work, and I had a young family to support. It was a tough time, but I needed to make this work for my family and for our future, so I rolled up my sleeves and got stuck in.

Together, my business partner and I cleaned. We did the hard graft together on everything from the business back end to the daily nitty gritty of putting on those cleaning gloves and getting the job done. It wasn't glamorous, by any means.

We began to set up systems and procedures, and we won contracts through door-to-door selling.

After six months we employed our first member of staff. Slowly but surely, we began to grow the business to the multimillion pound operation that it is today.

Whilst growing the cleaning business, I began to use my latent intuition again – that side of me that I had put aside for a while.

As time went by, it was an absolutely huge factor in our success. The more I tuned in to get guidance and the more I acted upon it, the more the business grew.

Having set my connection to Spirit aside, it all started back up again by using vision boards and setting goals to manifest, alongside my business partner, who was not at all into all this 'woo woo' stuff. At the time, *The Secret*, by Rhonda Byrne, was making big waves in the personal development and spiritual space, so manifesting was becoming quite commonplace, and we set about making our own dreams come true.

We would set goals, create vision boards, and set our intentions.

Every single goal we set, we hit.

After the success with manifesting, I'd pull cards, or begin to ask my guides for answers and guidance. I always made decisions using my 'gut' feeling, and of course Spirit often gave me a helping hand.

On one occasion, we turned up to one of my client's offices as usual, and I just felt this very strange, dark feeling wash over me.

I turned to my business partner, and said, "Something's not right. We won't be getting paid for this job. We need to leave now."

So we did.

The following day, I rang around to ask about the client, and it transpired that the business had gone that day. It had all been very sudden, and no-one was getting paid – but I knew, instinctively.

Trusting my gut, connecting to my higher self, and asking for guidance was such a key part to the success of the cleaning business.

Being from a family of butchers, and proper Northern, working class stock, I was raised to believe that you only got money through hard work; if you wanted something, then you had to work for it.

Money to me meant security, and if you didn't work hard then you would lose it, so I always put in effort over and above to make things work.

I truly believe that working with Spirit and manifesting with the Universe added another dimension to the huge success we achieved with the business. Hard work and trusting my gut was a winning combination.

Being tapped back into this ability and being able to use it to build a business and security for my family meant I could see a real-life use for this inner knowing.

Knowing things as a kid is one thing, but being able to fast track a business by trusting my gut, working with Spirit, and knowing the best choices to make, meant I could see a tangible reason to open up the magic box of tricks again.

I truly believe that we all have this ability.

We can all clear the spaces around us and within to be able to receive guidance, and this book will help you to do just that.

The success of my cleaning business from listening to the nudges along the way, means I have been able to harness my gifts and connection with Spirit on a much deeper level.

When I reopened that connection to Spirit, it was quite an assault on my energy field.

And I had to learn to protect myself, and go back to basics.

So often I would find myself feeling exhausted or faint, especially in large public places with lots of people. I had to learn to shut down my receptivity, because what I didn't realise at the time was that all kinds of energy was floating around me, and I just didn't know how to control it, so I was feeling totally drained.

I went to various events and workshops for psychic connection, and at one such event found myself connected with a wonderful medium who became my mentor. Over six months she taught me how to meditate, how to go into past lives, and how to recognise and connect to my mother. She was absolutely phenomenal, and a huge part of my own journey.

Right now, I am a full time Spiritual Coach and Energy Clearer. But it wasn't until the pandemic hit, that I fully threw myself into building a career as a medium, crystal healer, meditation teacher and spiritual coach.

The pandemic was a time of global reset for us all, and it was certainly the case for me.

I enjoyed reading for clients and they often came to me to gain closure or peace following a loved one's passing. I even wrote a book in 2013 on *How to Be Your Own Medium* to show to others that we all have the ability to communicate with Spirit, if you are open to it.

But from 2020, the guidance came through loud and clear that it's time – time to step up and to share my message about the CLEAR Method and communicating with Spirit to a much wider audience. And here we are, together in the pages of this book.

The CLEAR Method has always been there for me – it just took a little of my own medicine to determine what it is I actually do! It was when I realised the synchronicities of my Clairvoyant gifts (Clairvoyant – in French it means clear seeing - and the name I landed on CLEAR – it was meant to be shared.

One thing I am good at is clearing and cleaning. In fact, if you put a cloth in my hand I can't stop!

It might not look like this on the surface, but I am a self-confessed introvert. Though once you get to know me, the shyness fades away.

I would also say I am quite direct. I am Northern, after all. My daughter would say, I'm very bossy and also quite nosey! I have always been interested in people, what makes them tick, and how and why they behave the way they do.

I'm always keen to try and sort things out for people. However, the older I get, the more I have realised that people need to sort out their own issues, and I have more boundaries in place now.

To be honest, I'm often confused as to why people carry on doing the same things, in the same way expecting a different outcome. My standard line is, "If nothing changes, then nothing changes."

That said, I truly believe that we are *all* intuitive, and that being a psychic or a medium is not a gift, but an ability that we all have.

I absolutely love to teach people how to harness their intuition to live a successful life.

It is a passion of mine to help people to clear their energy blocks, so that they can access their intuition and trust in themselves to make the right decisions.

Energy blocks can come in all shapes and sizes, whether its energy you are carrying around with you, or your home is hoarding old energy that should be cleansed and cleared out. I think that's why being a cleaner was a natural first career, I love to clean and declutter a space and allow the fresh new energy in.

I even have a visualisation I do regularly on myself where I imagine a small version of myself vacuuming all the debris and energy that is not mine from each chakra, which I then empty into the ether to be transmuted. It's something that you might like to try too, and it's really easy to do... to grab it just visit my website www.carolyncreel.com

Often during readings, I'll sense that the client needs to clear some physical space in their home to allow the new to come in. After having a sort out or reorganising their spaces, clients will tell me that simply by decluttering on various levels they have been able to listen to their own intuition, and to begin trusting in themselves.

Spirituality can help people live a calmer life, a better life, and realise what's important.

The CLEAR Method is my way of helping you connect with your spirituality, from a very practical starting point.

From doing this work, I've had people walk away from relationships that didn't work, change their jobs, move countries and completely change their lives.

Often people say it's because of what I've said, but it's really not. They just needed a bit of coaxing.

I never, *ever* tell anybody what they don't already know. And that's what you will discover too, as we meander through these pages together, sweeping up areas of your life that need a little gentle (or not too gentle!) attention.

So that's me. I went from cleaning offices to helping people declutter their lives and connect to their spiritual gifts.

My journey has been full of twists and turns, and I am sure yours will be, too.

I am so happy to be with you right now, as the CLEAR Method helps you to begin clearing out space for your life to become even more amazing.

And because I'm nosey I'd love to hear how you get on!

Find me on Instagram @carolynspiritual

Get in the CLEAR Zone

Beginning Your CLEAR Journey

"...But it's then, then that faith arrives
To make your feelings alive
And that's why, you should keep on aiming high
Just seek yourself and you will shine
...You've got to search for the hero inside yourself
Search for the secrets you hide
Search for the hero inside yourself
Until you find the key to your life."
— Search for the Hero Inside Yourself: M People

As we begin this work together, imagine we are on a game board a little bit like the Game Of Life. For those of you that had children in the 80s or perhaps were a child of the 80s this will make sense to you.

After all, life *is* just like that game board, isn't it?

We move through different stages, we roll the dice, and we see different stages of life through a different lens, as we move through each one.

This book will support you through life stages, whether it's your children leaving home, grief, divorce, bereavement; or perhaps when you're just having kids and starting out in your new home, maybe you are just beginning your career and finding a job.

Perhaps you are older, looking at a new phase of life in your autumn years, starting a new business, maybe, just like I did.

Take a moment just to consider what it is you would love to gain from the CLEAR Method. Know that it might change each time you go through this book.

Maybe you're looking for a bit of clarity to manifest your ideal career and to call in your partner and your family.

Maybe you are looking for support and guidance from your higher self or from the Universe, as you navigate some of the midlife challenges that happen, whilst juggling kids and elderly parents.

Maybe you are at a crossroads in your life, and just need to know where to take the next step.

Whatever it is, take a moment just to feel how you would love this book to help you as you start, knowing that it might change each time you open these pages.

This is all about taking responsibility for yourself and your spaces – your mental, physical, spiritual, and emotional spaces.

When we do that, some really powerful things begin to shift, I promise you.

So wherever you are now in the game of life, this is your CLEAR Method starting point for right now.

This is your ground zero and the point from which you will measure, experience and centre celebrate the tangible incredible changes that are coming your way.

> "The truth will set you free, but first it will piss you off."
> – Joe Klaas, Twelve Steps to Happiness

Make notes under each of these sections, and help yourself to orientate where you are right now as you begin your CLEAR Method adventure.

You could use a journal to do this, or answer right here in the book – whatever feels the most supportive for you right now.

CLEAR Method Audit

Question 1:

As I begin my CLEAR Method journey I am most looking for clarity on:

Question 2:

The most challenging situation in my life right now is:

Question 3:

I would love to feel clearer in the following areas:

Question 4:

Who is the person I am becoming? How will I know when I am feeling progress?

The CLEAR Dance Space

When I think about the CLEAR Method, it reminds me of these five circles interlinking, like the diagram below, constantly connected, each one dancing in each other's spaces.

So parts of this book, whilst linear, it's also like one big dancing spiral. The idea of dancing fills me with joy, as I love a little boogie along with some Northern soul when I am in the decluttering zone.

Starting with Cleansing and Clearing, is often a great place to begin, but you may find yourself jumping into other areas.

Just know that there is no wrong way to do this, if you follow your own inner knowing and intuition along the way.

It may be that you start decluttering and clearing, say for example, it's baby clothes, or pictures from your kids' childhood. Now in 10 years' time when they are older, they may wish to discard those pictures keeping only one or two, but as a parent you feel you need to hold on to them, for them to make that decision. This is totally normal, and is probably what the majority of our parents' lofts are filled with!

So, what do you do?

You tidy those things away to lofts or shoeboxes under the bed to be cleared or released at a later date. That is totally normal and I wouldn't expect you to find it easy to discard treasures from your children. There will come a time when you find it easy to let go of things and time is the healer here.

I am not asking you to get rid of everything.

Maybe you aren't ready to Let Go... yet.

It might be you are energised because you have moved the memories to somewhere you can't see them, but still feel the comfort of knowing that they are there for the moment.

Maybe your house and mind is clear, and Receiving is where you need to begin your journey with me.

Whatever happens, this is a beautiful dance; moving through seasons and cycles just like Mother Nature, and this will ebb and flow with your own seasons and cycles.

Rituals and CLEARing

You may find as you work with the CLEAR Method and the energy of it – because as mad as it sounds, this does have an energy of its own as you'll discover! – that you develop your own set of habits around it, almost like rituals.

From the performance and sports science world, we know that rituals considered by others to be woo, are considered part of the brain's rewiring to improve performance. Remember, I'm one woo not two. I mean, I'm woo enough to speak to Spirit after all, but creating a ritual doesn't need to be some kind of candle burning, full moon ceremony. Although to be fair, if you'd like to let go of stuff under the Full Moon, that's the perfect time.

Rather, this is about creating sets of habits that work for you and for the way that you are CLEARing.

For example, you might discover that using a certain cloth or scent, or putting on a particular playlist really helps you to get into the zone.

You might find that letting go happens at certain times of either the month, the year, or your own internal cycle.

You might find that energising has a particular set of behaviours and rituals that really work for you. For example, always putting on a certain playlist, opening the windows and dancing, before you take something to a charity shop or to the dump. Or maybe you absolutely love the Purdy and Fig Vetiver spray, and you use that every time you have completed a clear out of your kitchen, for example.

Maybe you set aside some time in your diary or your calendar for your clearing and decluttering. and you listen to podcasts or audiobooks or things that really lift you up.

You will discover, as many of my clients have, that using the CLEAR Method becomes something that you look forward to, and an act of self-care rather than just something else on your to-do list.

Every time we take space in our lives to move energy around, to improve our spaces – our energetic, emotional, physical spaces – it really is something that makes our lives better. I promise you, no matter how resistant you might feel as you start this method and this book, if you can view it through the lens of looking after yourself and those around you, and (dare I even say) make it fun, this becomes something that you look forward to.

Jeanne, who is a client you will meet often in the book, had real resistance to decluttering and to clearing. It all felt completely overwhelming. In fact, she was also dealing with clutter in her Mum's house. Her Mum was a lifelong hoarder, and although her home was nowhere near like that, it felt like an extra chore to do these things in her own house.

She was a full time working mother of two and also battled chronic health conditions, so it always felt like an extra job.

But, when she started putting 15 minute chunks of time on her calendar every day, she found that she looked forward to those moments. She would put on some music that she loved, she would listen to podcasts, or audiobooks as she pottered around the house.

She soon found that she would do more than one 15 minute slice in one day, and ended up flying through her decluttering To Do list, and much to her surprise, also looked forward to it each time.

Over time she invested in some products that made her feel happy as she used them. As she embarked upon the CLEAR Method, she felt the effects really, really quickly.

The ritual for her became around looking forward to that time in her diary to be away from phone calls, friends, or family and to just to use it as a meditative practice.

Some days she turned up the music really loud and just enjoyed clearing her space and energising her home and her body. Some days it was a much quieter, mindful activity.

It might be different for you.

But whatever it is, finding your own way to CLEAR will be really important in this journey.

Get in the CLEAR Zone Quiz

How much stagnant energy are you hoarding?

First, I want to recognise that it does take time to CLEAR. When we hold onto memories, hand me downs, old photographs in the physical; by doing that we are also collecting energy.

Some good energy, some toxic or even energy that isn't ours. When we cleanse, let go of the old, energise, and take action we are then open to receiving the new.

The beauty of the CLEAR Method is it can be applied in every area of your life – physically, and energetically.

Check out my quiz to see where you could be holding onto energy that is no longer needed in your life.

Questions

1 - You walk into your house after a busy day. What's the first thing you see?

    A - Piles of newspapers, jars and boxes – 'just in case,' you know!

    B - Nothing! But the cupboards have a hazard warning...

    C - Shoes and clothes strewn all over the floor, piles of letters and notes to yourself.

    D - The ugly old vase that also happens to be a family heirloom, that you daren't get rid of.

    E - Cluttered sideboards and cupboards bursting at the hinges, you step over unknown things just to put the kettle on.

F - A nice clean, tidy, organised house.

G - Nothing! Your space is always a clean slate.

2 - It's a week after your birthday. What do you do with the box of chocolates you were given and birthday cards, now it's over?

A - You eat the chocolates and keep the box 'just in case' you need it.

B - You put the box in the back of the cupboard and forget it's there.

C - You start adding to the piles of recycling that stay on the sideboard in your kitchen – a work in progress, you know!

D - You store the box and the cards in your 'prosperity box' which is full of old birthday cards, ticket stubs and keepsakes from birthday's past.

E - The box just gets dropped on the floor with everything else.

F - You recycle responsibly after enjoying the chocolates and the cards, and leave no trace.

G - What chocolates? I re-gifted them, and the clean space is the real birthday present for me.

3 - It's your college reunion coming up, and you take a trip down memory lane.

A - You have kept all the photos, negatives, letters from friends, and mementos – you could take them to the reunion and share some memories.

B - You know those boxes in the attic have some juicy throwbacks, if only you could get to them..

C - Oh! That pile you were starting to sort out in the office must have some brilliant pictures.

D - You find yourself immersed in the memories as you go through the boxes of reports and photos from age of 5 to now, forgetting you are even looking for college stuff.

E - You have all the things from all the years, but trying to find them gives you the cold sweats – there's no point even trying.

F - You have a lovely photo of your favourite friend group displayed where you can see it and have happy memories.

G - You have taken photos of your photographs and stored them digitally, all labelled with dates, no paper footprints here, it's all about living in the moment.

4 - Your child is turning sweet 16.

A - You present them with a box containing all their birthday cards since they were born, along with baby teeth and their belly button clip (just in case).

B - You are pretty sure you have a memento to gift them, but daren't delve into the cupboards.

C - You have birthday cards, and notes to yourself in various piles around the house. (Hopefully no-one will have moved them!)

D - You have been adding every year to a huge box with their name on in the attic – clothes, baby teeth, artwork, letters, photos. It's a labour of love.

E - You are sure the gifts are here somewhere. But you have no hope of finding them.

F - You go immediately to your tickler file, and find the cards and gifts you purchased ahead of time.

G - Time together is a gift – we share experiences to make memories, objects don't matter.

5 - You have a big meeting in London tomorrow, and you are winding down for the day. How do you prepare yourself?

A - You have three outfits of clothing ready to wear, you've checked the train times, you have three pairs of shoes lined up, and you have pre-planned the route, depending on the weather – all sorted!

B - You should probably put on a meditation to de-stress right now, and you'll deal with what tomorrow brings when you wake up.

C - You know where everything is, you know what time your train is, and with help from your angels, if no-one gets in my way, you'll be fine and on time.

D - Tomorrow? You are still thinking about the thing that upset you on Monday, and can't stop your mind from whirring.

E - You are totally overwhelmed and shattered from the day, all the tabs are open, and where exactly is the music coming from?

F - You have just journaled your successes from today, you are calm and clear and prepared for tomorrow and whatever it may bring.

G - You are settling down to cleanse and clear your chakras, meditate, release and let go. Tomorrow is a brand new day.

6 - How do you keep your mind and body active?

A - You have a gym membership, sometimes use it, but keep spare trainers under your desk.

B - Is that something people do?

C - You have lists of local Pilates and yoga classes alongside your gym cards somewhere in a pile in your kitchen, and meditate when you remember.

D - You used to love dancing. It's been a while since you threw some shapes..

E - Takeaways and Netflix box set until 1am...

F - Your fitness regime mirrors your cycle, and all your downtime and yoga classes are scheduled on your calendar.

G - You listen to your body. It's a compass to let you know whether it needs walking, yoga, wild swimming, or rest. Anything is possible.

If you Answered...

Mainly answered A - Just in Case.

Whether it's memories, energy or things, you store things from the past in case you need to return to them.

Perhaps it's time to review with fresh eyes to see what 'just in case' could be used for right now, or moved on.

Mainly answered B - Out of sight, out of mind.

You love to give the impression you have everything organised on the surface. But open up those cupboards and who knows what you've crammed in there.

I'm a great believer that your space is a reflection of your energy field, where do you need to go deeper?

Mainly answered C - Organised chaos.

You know where everything is. It's just in that pile over there. Trouble is no-one else does. This is great until you need to involve others.

So maybe consider taking an hour or two out of your week to sort and minimise the chaos. It's a useful exercise and you could even involve family members so you aren't the 'go to' for everything.

Mainly answered D - Can't let go.

Often we hold on to items, things, and energy that no longer serves us. The trouble is when we do that it gets heavy in every way.

What do you need to let go of? What are you holding on to that no longer serves you? These questions are worth sitting with and perhaps journaling on, before you physically start to CLEAR.

Mainly answered E - I haven't seen my floor in decades.

It's so easy to get here, isn't it? One minute you can see the floor and the next you just give up because it seems like too big a task.

My mantra is, 'A tidy space, reflects a tidy mind.' By taking baby steps to cleanse and clear your physical space and ultimately your mind, you will be surprised how much clearer things become.

Perhaps start with one room or drawer at a time. Give yourself a goal to tackle one thing each day, however small.

Mainly answered F - Everything has its place.

Well congratulations – a tidy space and a tidy mind!

Receiving is also one of the hardest things to do – when we have a clear space, clarity comes but often we find it hard to enjoy it. So, I do hope you find time to schedule in some time to enjoy your clear and receptive space.

Mainly answered G - I own nothing, I am free

Someone once said to me, "You can't take it with you."

I suspect you are living a life you love and I applaud you for that.

I hope you enjoyed my little quiz. Whilst it was designed as a little fun, I find it useful to help me pinpoint where my efforts could be well spent.

C is for Clear,
Cleanse and Clarity

'The first thought...
is the best thought"

Carolyn Creel

C is for Clear, Cleanse and Clarity

"She's living in a world and it's on fire
Filled with catastrophe, but she knows she can fly away."
Girl on Fire – Alicia Keys

So, let's get started on your CLEAR journey. As I mentioned earlier on, often the Clean and Let Go, go hand in hand. But there are some basic 'jobs' you can get started with.

In this chapter, I cover every area of your life you may need to declutter and offer tips, guidance and my own stories.

We will take a look at every area of your life and determine where you need to declutter.
- The Physical – our homes, personal space and body
- The Mind – declutter thoughts
- Our Connections / Relationships – friendships, love interests, family
- Major Life Events – Birth / Death / Move home / Marriage / Divorce.

But first let's connect a little deeper with what is niggling you right now to CLEAR?

Our Physical Spaces are an Extension of Self

I often say our homes and spaces are a reflection of our minds and an extension of us.

When we went through the quiz together earlier, you may have an idea of the places you need to tackle first.

I liken the rooms of a house as a mirror to your energy field. If you are into 'woo' – you'll know all about the Chakras.

For those of you who don't; Chakras are energy centres within our physical bodies. Each coloured Chakra represents a different area of the body.

The Chakra is defined as a spinning wheel of energy that runs up the spine to the top of the head. Concepts of the seven Chakras came to the Western world in the 1880s from yoga and Reiki practices from the East.

Energy workers like myself work with the energy centres to help people clear emotional and energetic blockages.

I've included a diagram below which gives you a basic premise of where each Chakra is and what it relates to in life.

THE SEVEN CHAKRAS
AND THEIR MEANINGS

SAHASRARA — "I UNDERSTAND"
CROWN CHAKRA — KNOWLEDGE & CONSCIOUSNESS

AJNA — "I SEE"
THIRD EYE CHAKRA — INTUITION & LUCIDITY

VISHUDDHA — "I TALK"
THROAT CHAKRA — COMMUNICATION & CREATIVITY

ANAHATA — "I LOVE"
HEART CHAKRA — LOVE & SINCERITY

MANIPURA — "I DO"
SOLAR PLEXUS CHAKRA — STRENGTH & DETERMINATION

SVADHISHTHANA — "I FEEL"
SACRAL CHAKRA — SENSUALITY & PLEASURE

MULADHARA — "I AM"
ROOT CHAKRA — ENERGY & STABILITY

The whole reason we CLEAR on all levels – our homes, our physical beings and our relationships – is because we are all energy and our connections to others, the spaces we reside in, all play a part.

The clearer our energy field and our spaces, the more receptive we become.

I believe our homes have a Chakra system too; because they are essentially an extension of us.

When our minds and spaces are cluttered and stuck, WE are cluttered and stuck.

You only have to look up other cultures who put this into regular practice – the art of Feng Shui for example – who see this as part of life. The Pagan rituals of old – for example our spring cleaning always began around Spring Equinox;

or harvesting was celebrated around Autumn Equinox – also speak into this. When we work with seasons and cycles of the year it, in itself, brings about different tasks we can all integrate into daily life fairly easily. And some of us may be doing it unconsciously in any case.

So onto the Chakras...

Our Root Chakra is in essence our home. This represents our survival, where we feel safe, basic needs of having a roof over our heads and food on our table. When this is balanced in our bodies and in our home, we feel safe and secure and confident. In the home, this is the kitchen, and bathroom where we take care of our basic human needs.

I would also go so far as to mention the loft - yes it does get forgotten – because it's often where we store all our memories from the past. I've got a story about that too...

Our Sacral Chakra represents the space of creativity and sexuality; I would suggest that our bedrooms are a reflection of this chakra. Often as children, we play games in our bedrooms and as we move into adulthood our bedrooms become a place of creation in other ways... no, you're blushing...!

Our Solar Plexus represents the space of wisdom. And in the body it is found in our digestive areas. It's where we hold our stress-related illnesses and stomach issues. You could link this Chakra to the key living spaces where we eat and consume each other's energy like the kitchen, dining room and the lounge.

Our Heart Chakra is what it says on the tin. It is representative of the Heart of home. In the physical home, again this is any shared living space and the people within it. If your family members are unbalanced in any way, then that can have an effect too and we will talk into that a little more later on.

Our Throat Chakra is located in the body at the base of the throat and represents communication and healthy expression. This in the home is where you talk and communicate with your family members and receive communication – so places where you listen to the radio or watch TV or converse with each other; so hallways, lounge and bedrooms.

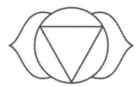

Our Third Eye Chakra is our connection to our intuition and inner knowing. On the body, it is situated between our eyebrows. When this is imbalanced in our bodies we can experience headaches and blurred vision. When it's balanced we become free of the fear of death and remain free of attachment to material things. In the home, this for me links to anywhere there is clutter – loft, cupboards, anything where we are holding on to material things we no longer need.

Our Crown Chakra is located in the crown of the head in the body and is the centre of dynamic thought and energy. When imbalanced you can suffer from frustration, melancholy and restlessness. A balanced Crown Chakra brings about peace with a clear perspective. It also brings about the strong emotion of letting go and also the joy of transformation.

In our homes, this isn't a room as such – more a state of the home. I see this as a decluttered, clear space – so when our homes are free of things we no longer need we are clear and open to receive. When our Crown is balanced it's a great time to declutter the physical!

So now I have given you a crash course on Chakras and how that relates to the CLEAR Method, we can begin to Declutter your life.

CLEAR Your Home

If you answered the quiz earlier, and clutter in the home is something you realise you need to tackle, then this section is for you.

We can go gently.

Removing old energy and clearing your home of clutter doesn't need to be time-consuming or overwhelming.

It's all about starting small.

You don't want to turn your house upside down on the first go. That's tantamount to setting off the overwhelm.

So here's what I recommend to get you started and in the flow of shifting stagnant energy that could be festering in your home.

First schedule in five minutes per day in your calendar (or longer if you think you'll need it). Getting started is the important thing here.

And remember the black bags...

Five Minutes a Day for Seven days...

Day 1

Spend your five minutes (note this is extra to your usual chores); on decluttering an area where you spend the most time. This could be at your desk; or in your living room; clear out anything that doesn't need to loiter on the sideboard.

Day 2

Cleanse and clear out one drawer in your home. Pick a drawer, say the odds and bits drawer in your kitchen. You know the one, you've been meaning to get to for ages, you know the one full of bits and bobs... go tackle it.

Day 3

Clear where you sleep. Open the window, change your bedclothes, if you haven't already; and declutter your bedside table or that pile of books groaning next to your bed. Perhaps move your phone charger to another room, so you can start to declutter your mind by not having your mobile next to the bed. Did you know you spend most of your life asleep and in your bed? So it should be a clutter, and where possible, tech-free zone.

Day 4

Choose a cupboard. You choose the room, but pick a cupboard and use the same premise as you did with your drawer. Empty it, re-organise it, based on what you still need, and anything that hasn't seen the light of day for a while think long and hard over whether you still need it sat in that cupboard. Rule of thumb, if you haven't used it for 3-6 months, it could be time to move it on, recycle or bin it!

Day 5

Pick a room that you and your family spend a lot of time in; clear the surfaces, put away those items of clothing hanging around; have a tidy round. Then open the windows; and have a dance and sing around to change the energy of the room.

You'll be surprised how much better that room will feel to you and your family – better still get them to join in!

Day 6

Pick a wardrobe or drawer in your bedroom; bring a black bag with you. We hold so much energy in our clothes. We hold on to old clothes because they represent moments in the past we want to hold onto. So it's time to get ruthless with those jeans you have been hanging on to for four years. Or get rid of those greying knickers that are just clogging up your underwear drawer. Go through and pick out anything you haven't worn for a year. We can start slow. Hold the garment in your hand or try it on – see how it feels to you.

If it doesn't sit right, or it feels uncomfortable on your skin or just doesn't fit – it's time to recycle or sell on.

Day 7

Time to reflect. After a hard week of decluttering it's time to now reflect back on what you have achieved over the past six days...So I would love it if you could just sit with these questions and write down your thoughts as they come to mind.

CLEAR Journal Prompts

How do you feel?

How does the space feel around you?

Have you noticed a difference since you tackled that cupboard / drawer / wardrobe ?

And most importantly has it given you an appetite to do a little more decluttering in your home?

What is next?

Once you have sat with these questions, and you do have the appetite, keep working slowly and gently on each room or cupboard. Decluttering your home's chakras, working your way up to bigger tasks to places like the loft or that cupboard under the stairs!

And if there are items you are finding hard to let go of, put those to one side and we can explore this a little further in *L is for Letting Go*.

Let's Clean House

After you have decluttered your spaces, cleaning your house of residual dirt and energy is also very important.

Cleaning your home regularly can improve your health and mental wellbeing. And it also helps you to keep on top of dirt and germs.

I've tried and tested many ways, and it comes back to this each time. Homes and offices should be cleaned and decluttered regularly.

A surface clean should take place at a minimum of once a week, paying particular attention to bathrooms and kitchen areas.

Remember I mentioned those Chakras earlier on, the Root Chakra represents the areas that offer us security and are where our basic human needs are met (bathrooms / shower / toilets) so I would recommend paying particular attention to those.

Bathrooms / Showers / Toilets

As you are probably aware, bathrooms, specifically toilets, sinks and showers, are germ and infection breeding areas. The build-up of dead skin, body fats and hair can cause issues in sinks and showers drains, and if not kept on top of, can become extremely hard to shift especially in hard water areas.

There are lots of specific cleaning products for bathrooms out there, I personally suggest choosing a good disinfectant to kill all germs.

Then for windows, mirrors and glass, I would make up my own simple solution of water and white vinegar – 1:1 ratio of diluted vinegar and water and store it in a spray bottle. It's not only a great disinfectant, it also stops water stains and keeps them smear clear.

Another recommendation, to break down grease, body fats and skin build up is to use a neutral detergent or washing up liquid.

I'm a huge fan of a microfibre cloth to wipe down surfaces and I have a separate one for each room. These can then be washed on high temps and reused over and over again.

Toilets should be cleaned daily with a toilet brush; And then every few days pop toilet cleaner in and leave it for an hour before scrubbing under the rim and down into the u-bend, this ensures you keep on top of any infections passing between family members.

I would also suggest a thorough descale of toilets at least once a month, to stop the build-up of uric acid and limescale.

A girl's best friend is a plunger. To keep your shower healthy, check your shower drain once a week to remove any hair and skin build up, and stop the smells! Shower heads normally unscrew and can be left to soak in a dishwasher tablet or descaler to keep the water flowing through and it stops the build up!

And finally to keep the energy flowing in those spaces, I would highly recommend a plant. Plants are a fab way to re-oxygenate and energise a room. Choose a plant specific to the type of room – something that will thrive in damp spaces for bathrooms for example.

Kitchens

When it comes to kitchens, there is the inevitable build-up of grease and odours from cooking. If you don't clean up after yourself every time you visit the kitchen, then you risk picking up infection from food either not being properly cooked or cleaned up after.

My recommendation here is to clean surfaces daily with kitchen cleaner and change up your microfibre cloths, or better still allocate different coloured cloths for different jobs i.e. you won't want to use the cloth you used to clean the floor on your dinner plates.

Clean your hobs weekly; and go through your fridge once a month and clean it out with hot water and soapy water to minimise the harmful bacteria that can breed if you don't stay on top of it.

I would also suggest once every three months invest in an oven deep clean. Extractor fans can also carry a lot of grease, and just soaking the mesh in a hot sink of soapy water does the trick.

One other hack I can also recommend for sink plug holes, is putting a dishwasher tablet in the plughole and then pouring boiling water over it. This removes any stains, gets rid of stinky sinks and the inevitable germ build up.

And of course stay on top of your bins. Try not to let them overflow; and change your food bins daily; washing them regularly too!

Floors

I would recommend that to stay on top of skin flakes, dust bunnies and pet hair, you vacuum all floors right up to the skirting board on a regular basis. Then at least once a month, move sofas and get behind cupboards to stay on top of dust accumulation.

With hard floors, I would recommend you stick with a vacuum, before mopping, as brooms tend to move dust around. Mopping floors with disinfectant several times a week will keep your floors clean and germ free.

Bedrooms

Bedrooms are our space of rest. We spend half our lives in our beds and therefore this space gathers a lot of dust and (dare I say it, body fluids).

So change your bedding once a week, shake out your covers daily and open your windows first thing to allow the air to change. Declutter the spaces near your head – bedside cabinets only need a book and a lamp, and keep technology to a minimum.

Our wardrobes and cupboards become places where we hold on to old memories, whether its clothing or keepsakes.

These are spaces that can regularly get snarled up with clutter, so add these to the top of your list, and be mindful if there are things that you feel uncomfortable moving on. Set them aside, and we can revisit when ready.

Lounge / Dining Room / Hallway

Theses living spaces are places we all reside in and visit daily. So dust and clutter accumulates without you even noticing.

Opening the windows, cleaning spaces with microfibre cloths, decluttering surfaces and dusting photographs regularly are all important in keeping those spaces fresh and clear.

Washing cushion covers and any soft furnishings, curtains and nets, also help to keep on top of any germs that are lingering.

Hanging coats and putting shoes away should be done as you walk in the house, so you aren't trampling the outside in. Get the family to help and make them accountable for their own belongings.

Bottom line – Make it a fun daily ritual!

Clean and clear your home regularly.

Ditch the polish and the broom – you are just moving the dirt around and adding to the build-up. Use as few chemicals as possible. Water and microfibre cloths capture dust and dirt easily and effectively. And it's good for the environment too.

Clean your toilet, wash your dishes, declutter, and wipe round your surfaces daily.

Change your bedding and vacuum the whole house weekly.

If you don't clean and declutter your house regularly, you can attract all kinds of nasties such as ants, vermin, fleas or bedbugs.

One suggestion is to pick a day when you do your major jobs to start the week clean and clear.

Make it fun, or use it as an opportunity to empty your mind. It's surprising how doing jobs around the home can become meditative and help you to clear space in your head!.

I love to put on some tunes, dance and sing along, much to my daughter's despair – ha! But this helps to clear the energy of the space along with staying on top of the physical space. I'll cover this one for you in just a moment.

Keeping on top of those jobs will help you to ensure the energy flows through the Chakras of the home, inviting in new energy and possibilities.

CLEAR the Space

Once you have cleaned your physical home, you can then take steps to cleanse and clear the energetic imprint of a space. I referenced this in *Seven Steps to Decluttering Your Space*, but I wanted to share a little more about this.

Homes are like energetic sponges, they hold onto memories, happenings and past trauma, just like us.

Why do you think that there are the phenomena of haunted homes?

Now, I am not saying your home is haunted, but what I do believe is energy in the home can be cleansed and cleared so the occupant becomes more open to receiving goodness in their life.

There are some very basic rituals I can recommend that can be added to regular cleaning and cleansing of the home. Some may seem far out there and others more palatable.

Pick whichever feels good to you!

Love and appreciate your house – say hello and goodbye to your home. I like to visualise a colourful veil over my house to keep it protected.

Place rock salt or obsidian crystals in the corners of the rooms, to add a layer of protection and keep negative energy out.

Open and regularly clean your windows to let the light in. Imagine all the heavy energy flowing out and clear crisp light energy coming in.

Your space is your space, so when visitors pop round – burn essential oils, Palo Santo, sage or incense. Whilst doing this you can repeat these words or your own take... *"This house is clean and clear, leave your worries outside of here."* Then open windows and say, "Anything that is not mine please move on," which helps to remove any residual energy that may be lingering.

Bring positive, happy vibes to your home by singing and dancing around (yes, really!). Or, walk around the house clapping (noise is a great energy clearer); or invest in sound bowls or play some Binaural beats – you will find some lovely tracks on YouTube to bring sound healing into your home.

Animals are a great way to increase joy in a home. My dogs are great at breaking me out of a bad mood because they do not carry the worries of humans.

Bringing the outside in, is another natural and great way to help to cleanse and clear a space (especially if oils and Palo Santo isn't for you). House plants help to oxidise the space naturally; flowers can bring cheer and colour into a space.

Crystals and wind chimes are not just pretty to look at and lovely additions to the garden and home. They also help to clear the space, attracting the sun and allowing the wind to move through them. Sound is an excellent larger space clearer.

CLEAR Your Mind

We talk about decluttering the physical spaces around us, but what about within?

As an energy healer and psychic, and those who find themselves on a spiritual path, this is often where we start.

We learn how to cleanse and clear our own energy through many modalities including meditation, Reiki (or energy healing), ecstatic dance, crystal healing, breathwork and sound healing.

These are all fantastic ways of cleansing and clearing your energy field; and there are many teachers and guides who can support you, and teach you how to do this yourself eventually.

I would love to touch on a few quick and simple ways you can clear your mind, which will enable you to move on to the next section.

Hot Air Balloon Visualisation

First I'd like to invite you to sit in a quiet space and take several deep cleansing breaths.

Take three deep cleansing breaths; then imagine you are in a lovely green field.

You can see a hot air balloon. Its bright and colourful like a rainbow. You jump into the basket, and you notice coloured bags hanging off the side of the balloon.

I invite you to go to the Red coloured bag; this is representative of your Root Chakra. I invite you to release the Red bag over the side of the hot balloon. The balloon lifts slightly as you release the clutter and baggage that is residing in your Root Chakra, the space of security and wealth.

Then I invite you to move to the Orange coloured bag. This is representative of your Sacral Chakra. I invite you to release the

Orange bag over the side of the hot air balloon. The balloon lifts again, as you release the clutter and baggage that is residing in your Sacral Chakra; the space of creativity.

Then it's time to invite you to go to the Yellow coloured bag. This is representative of your Solar Plexus Chakra. I invite you to release the Yellow bag over the side of the hot air balloon. The balloon starts to lift further into the air, as you release the clutter and baggage that is residing in your Solar Plexus Chakra.

Hopefully by now you are getting the hang of it, but next move to the Green bag. This is representative of your Heart Chakra. I invite you to open and tip the contents of the Green bag over the side of the hot air balloon. The balloon moves higher into the sky as you empty the dust and clutter and baggage that is residing in your Heart Chakra.

Then move to the Blue coloured bag. This is representative of your Throat Chakra. I invite you to release the Blue bag over the side of hot air balloon. The balloon moving higher into the sky as you release the clutter and baggage that is residing in your Throat Chakra.

It's the Indigo coloured bag next. This is representative of your Third Eye Chakra. I invite you to release the Indigo bag over the side of the hot balloon. The Balloon lifts slightly as you release the clutter and baggage that is residing in your Third Eye Chakra.

And finally we reach the Crown. The final bag is white or gold, whichever feels right to you, and when you get to this bag, I would guide you to open the bag and tip the dust into the ether; as your balloon flies high into the sky!

After you have completed this meditation, you should feel clearer and more receptive.

Another way to help to declutter your mind before you start your day, (if meditation doesn't work for you) is as follows:

Morning CLEAR Ritual

Keep a journal or notepad by your bed; and each morning before you start anything, journal on the following questions:

- Clear – What is my intention and focus for the day?
- Let Go – What do I need to let slide/or let go of today?
- Energise – How can I energise myself today? What lights me up?
- Action – What three things need actioning today?
- Receive – What would I like to receive today?

CLEAR Your Life

What my personal experience as a psychic medium has shown me over the years is, more often than not, people visit me looking for answers.

They perhaps have a personal issue they need guidance on, and those personal issues more often than not fall in a few camps.

Those camps tend to be as follows:

- Family – immediate or those who have passed
- Love and Relationships – friendships or partners
- Money, career or job
- Health and wellbeing
- And of course major life events – birth, death, marriage, divorce, moving home

Now, I want to set a clear caveat here, because I am not by any means a psychologist or doctor. However, I do have many years of wisdom and insight shared by spirit over the years. If you need medical advice please seek the help of a qualified pro, now that's out the way, let's begin.

When clients visit, more often than not, the client's spirit team will show me that the person needs to clear space to think and gain clarity on what it is they are asking for guidance on. Especially as all our answers are already available to us. We just need to know where to look.

A clear home is an extension of your mind and energy field.

So more often than not, I will get guidance on sharing that particular person needs to declutter their bedroom or their loft.

They will go away and declutter that space, and will either fall upon something they had long forgotten; or realise they had physically held on to things or people that are no longer fit or needed.

I'll talk about this in more depth in the L segment of the book.

We literally can't take it with us, so why do we hold onto stuff so tightly? My theory is the most important things in life can be kept in a shoebox. Everything is memories and held in our mind.

I am also a great believer in the saying, *if nothing changes, then nothing changes*. This can be applied in pretty much every area of life.

So let's briefly look over the various areas of life that may need your attention in decluttering.

I invite you to be with your thoughts to see where your connections may need a spring clean or declutter.

CLEAR Your Connections Visualisation

I invite you to sit in a fairly clear space in your home to tune into what is coming up for you.

Take several deep grounding breaths to really drop into it.

Then I invite you to visualise you in the middle of all the connections around you.

What is coming up first? What is the first thing that springs to mind?

Is it a person; or a space in the home; your business or money?

Hold that first vision; and ask to go a little deeper into what is being shown to you.

> Explore that vision for as long as you need to, and don't be
> afraid to ask questions of what it is you need to do next.
>
> Then bring yourself back to the present through wiggling toes,
> moving your arms and bringing yourself back into the room.
>
> Now is a good time to see what came up for you.

Family

Now they always say you can't choose your family.

And I believe that we chose to be here, at this time, for a reason.

Often that reason is because we are here to break and heal old cycles and old patterns in our family lineage – deep, I know.

Often our arguments or discomfort with family members stems from something more.

Maybe one of you is holding onto something in the past.

My Mum for example put everything she no longer needed in the loft, and I am not afraid to share that I struggled at times to understand her motivation in life. But as I grew up and became more conscious; I could see that she married my Dad very young, so she 'grew up' with my Dad. Almost parenting her at times.

She liked to collect things and so when she moved, we found literally a whole house in the loft which my sister and I were tasked with clearing. It was acting like a huge block; kind of like when you are so overwhelmed you just can't cram anything else into that space. So when we had essentially removed the whole other house stuffed up in the loft, we all felt that sense of clarity. My sister and I were able to dump a lot of those old memories kept in the loft fairly easily.

One thing I realise now, is Mum's journey was her's. No amount of telling her or trying to get her to change made any difference. She could be difficult and attention seeking and childish. And for a long time, I thought I was the issue. But now I realise, whilst we blame ourselves, the biggest take away with family is to recognise it is not ours to fix or heal. They are on their own journey and sometimes just getting clarity and acceptance is enough.

When it comes to family, sometimes there is a need to declutter your thought patterns, and invite in new ones.

When we move into different stages of life for example, we can find ourselves sitting in a space with an old version or story about someone – often your child, partner or parent.

For example, Sandra, one of my clients, was having a few issues with her husband, as both of them had got stuck in old thought patterns and behaviours. When we met I shared with her that perhaps she needed to approach her husband and have a conversation about the things that were firing her up. She was desperate to move or decorate – the pandemic left her feeling fed up with her house. And it was a cycle she had found herself in multiple times.

She had already decided he would be against both those ideas, as he hadn't had the inclination to change anything even though he too hated the house. I could see clearly she was stuck in an old loop. Both of them (husband and wife) were perfectly capable of having the conversation and changing their ending, they just needed to approach it differently to how they had done in the past – slanging match and snatching conversations over their children – cue no time for approaching it calmly.

This old thought pattern/way of approaching their issue needed to be decluttered to enable them both to move forwards. What Sandra had also disclosed to me was she had already begun decluttering the room that was really frustrating her – the lounge – so she had already begun unconsciously making space for the new.

It turns out after I shared my guidance with her, Sandra realised two things were true:

1. Her husband was extremely busy at work and didn't have the bandwidth to think about Sandra's ideas for the home, especially during the day when he was working.

2. Sandra had begun the necessary preparation to begin changing the space; and just needed to voice her ideas at a time that worked for them both, not during her husband's working hours and definitely not when the kids were around and both were tired.

So Sandra, seeing the old pattern she needed to cleanse and clear, decided to approach it differently – more on that in a wee while.

One thing that does come up regularly in my readings, is that we women often think men have the foresight to pick up on what is bothering us.

Hate to break it to you – but they really don't. *And the same can be said for us too...*

Well you may have read Men are from Mars, Women are from Venus?

It still rings true.

Open communication is THE decluttering tool in any relationship, especially with our close family members and life partners.

Another thing to add is that our blokes don't ever appear to notice physical clutter.*

Does your guy or son constantly walk past the washing basket left at the bottom of the stairs?

Or leave out plates and cups next to the draining board?

Does he have a drawer full of jumpers he either keeps for best or can't let go of?

Our men deal with clutter in a very different way to women.

They will either ignore it and step over it, or remove it immediately when they remember.

They don't appear to hoard as much as women (physically or emotionally), though apparently they do love a jam jar or shed to keep their nik naks in... so I could be wrong?

There seems to be no middle ground, certainly with the guys I have come across. And one thing is certain, they tend not to suddenly start cleaning or doing jobs around the house on a whim.

They will muck in, however, IF you ask them... (!) so ladies stop nailing yourself to the cross!

Unfortunately, it is just not something that comes naturally to some men (and women aren't great at asking) – because it has always in the past been women's work. Though this is changing it can still run deep.

*Note – these are observations based on the client's and men I know, so this may not be applicable to all men. And well done you for finding a guy who bucks the old school patterns)

Anyway, back to Sandra and her husband.

So, when Sandra managed to get her husband out of the house, without the kids and away from the pressures of work, she was able to put across her proposal to decorate. Instead of being shut down; Husband was open to the changes and even suggested they go sofa shopping and decorate it together while he was on holiday.

The result of approaching the ask, once the groundwork had been done, meant Sandra not only got to declutter her physical space, but they are working as a team on changing their living space together. Which in turn has brought them both closer together.

Another example of this is around siblings or our children. Sometimes we can find ourselves stuck in the past, repeating an old cycle from our childhood or theirs.

So with that in mind, I would love to invite you to grab a journal or a piece of paper to do what I like to call a 'CLEAR Self-Assessment.' We'll also add these in the Action section of the book for easy access too!

CLEAR Self-Assessment – Family

Think about your close family relationships to see where you (or they) could be stuck in the past, who comes to the forefront of your mind when you ponder on this?

When you look at your child, do you still see them as an infant? By that I mean, do you still baby your child, do things for them they perhaps can do themselves?

When you look at your siblings, do you find yourself revisiting a time when you were younger? When your sister stole your favourite shoes and returned them damaged? Or your brother used to pick on you in front of his friends.

When you look at your parents, what memories come up for you? Are they still perhaps treating you like a young adult?

Often these stuck records occur when you are shifting into new phases of life, when you give birth, when your child leaves school or college, when your child moves into being more independent.

And often these thoughts and glitches in our family relationships just need to be recognised, cleared and let go of.

Love and Relationships - Friendships and Dating

This is probably the biggest area that comes up in readings and possibly one of the trickiest. I have already alluded to some of this in the family section, especially in relation to decluttering our relationships with a life partner or husband or wife.

Of course, this continues to relate to the Heart Chakra; and is primarily about connection, communication and self-appreciation.

One thing I often get asked about, is about other people. And often the guidance is to look after number one, which I am under no illusion can be difficult if your friendships have been a little one sided... just know that everything will fall into place.

Friendships are places we also grow out of. And because we are conditioned to hold onto things, people also fall into this category.

Now I probably sound a little harsh, I did warn you... but we do have a tendency to collect friendships especially in our teens and 20s. This is completely understandable, we create friendship groups at school, in college and in our first jobs. These are the places where we are learning about ourselves and are gravitating to people who have something in common with us at that point in our life.

It might be even now, you have an old school friend you are friends with but literally the only thing you have in common is to wander down memory lane talking about what you got up to as kids. And that's OK. As I've said before, it's OK to visit the past, but don't hang around there. So when you look at friendships you have around you, how are they serving you? Are they lifting you up? Are they cheering you on? Do they undermine you or make you feel small or silly?

And another thing to reference here, in this age of social media and digital connection, how many 'friends' do you have on Facebook or TikTok? There is this tendency to collect followers on these spaces as well. And you may or may not realise but each connection in the digital space is also energetic. When these spaces first started there was a desire to have more friends than the next one, a popularity contest if you will. But now the fancy with some of these platforms is subsiding. You may find your energy is hanging out with old crowds and these can be causing energetic leaks or affecting your clarity. My advice here is to regularly review your social spaces, and remove your energy from friendships and connections who no longer serve you.

The same could be said for love and dating; we talked a little into Sandra's story, as I see that as more of an established family member. But what about when you are looking for that special someone; or are seemingly unlucky in love.

This is a question or focus for many of my clients when they visit me. Frequently, the first thing I am asked is, "Is he or she the one?"

Often these doubts are compounded in a feeling or a knowing. Essentially, if you have to ask me that question, you will already know the answer. Now I'm not a trained psychologist, but I do have some thoughts on this. If the person you are enquiring about isn't being kind overall, or treating you with respect, I would always suggest that they are not the one.

But humans are complicated beings and we sometimes get blindsided by words and behaviours.

All I can really say on this is, trust your own inner judgement, hold onto your power and stay rooted in the belief that you deserve love – and you cannot go far wrong.

So with that in mind, and because ultimately I cannot tell you what to do, I can, however guide you to look in the right place.

To declutter those relationships that no longer serve you, sit with the following questions and see what comes up for you.

Self-Assessment – Friendships and Connections

Do you feel stuck with some of your friendships?

Are there friends in your life who you haven't heard from in over a year?

Do you feel invisible to some friends?

Do you do all the running in some friendships?

Are you clinging onto friendships from school or college just because you feel you should?

What are your Social Media channels like? Are you collecting old friends or do you regularly cull those you no longer see in real life?

Speaking about Facebook for a minute, when you post does it feel uncomfortable – are you worried about what certain people will think when they see what you are sharing? If so, are they truly your friends now? Little suggestion, these are probably the people you should mute or unfriend.

Do you check up on old friends – or lurk in the past? Perhaps ask yourself why you are doing that? What needs to be decluttered so you can move into clarity?

Self-Assessment on Love

These questions are a little more specific to those people looking for love.

Are you having a hard time holding a relationship down?

Do you find it hard to attract love?

What traits would you wish to see in an ideal partner?

Are you looking for love or lust?

What do you want from a partner?

Do you check up on old loves on Facebook – do you find it hard to get closure?

How do you feel about yourself?

Often when we are struggling to attract our life partner it is because we need to declutter our own thoughts about ourselves. To truly attract someone who is aligned with you, it starts with making sure you know who you are, and you love who you are.

Money - Business or Job

I am a great believer in the saying, "If nothing changes, then nothing changes."

This can be applied in pretty much every area of life, especially when it comes to our jobs and how we make money. My success came with a mix of blood, sweat and tears; and listening to my intuition or gut instincts. The more I tuned into those instincts the more abundant the business became.

Money has a bad press; there are so many old stories about money – 'You have to work hard to earn good money,' for example. Many of my clients come to me asking about their careers; because it is critical to live in today's society.

To declutter this area of your life, it's important to regularly check in with yourself and ask yourself the following questions, probably every three months. Kind of like a personal performance review.

Self-Assessment on Business or Job

So, how is your work situation right now?

Are you generally happy with the work you do?

Do you enjoy the work?

Is there anything you don't enjoy doing?

Where can you clear out any unnecessary clutter in your business, or job?

And to take this a step further, do you have a crowded desk or mailbox? Are you cluttering up your emails with old emails from two years ago?

Are you on top of where your money is going? Do you know what your money is spent on?

Are you spending money on old memberships you no longer need?

Can you review contracts with mortgages, energy providers to make them go further for you?

Is there anything you decluttered from the home that can be sold on to add more fluidity to your cash flow?

Money and our career is also connected to our Root Chakra. When this is functioning as it should, then you will have more than enough money to keep a roof over your head and for your basic human needs.

Health

Again I'd like to stress I am not a doctor or health expert. But I do have common sense, and as an energy worker, it makes complete sense to treat your body as a sacred vessel that houses your energy.

I mean, you regularly service your car, why not declutter your health habits?!

To enable you to gain clarity of thought, it is important to put the right amount of fuel in your body. I am not saying go vegan, what I am saying is balance and moderation.

Sometimes your body will want a glass of wine, sometimes you might want that slice of chocolate cake, or puff on a ciggie!

Like your house, as I mentioned earlier, your body is tuned to old patterns and traumas too. So, before you pour that glass or reach for the cake, I would suggest you check in with your body first to see what it is trying to tell you.

Now I am not trying to make you feel guilty about any unhealthy habits, but that's just it, isn't it? We normally know when we are making unhealthy choices for ourselves – our body certainly lets us know in some way.

Another thing to note is, when we shift into the winter of our lives, that is when a lot of our unhealthy choices catch up with us. So the sooner you can make some tweaks that stick the better for you!

I mean menopause can be a bitch if you continue to treat your body like it's 20 still. Personally, I saw how my mother and sister suffered with their sweats, and I decided that wasn't going to happen to me. So I adjusted my habits accordingly cutting out sugar, caffeine and booze. I still enjoy those things, but not to the level I once perhaps did.

"You are in control, it doesn't control you."

Again I would never tell you what to do, I can just share what I know and am guided to share.

I would love to throw the line of questioning back to you to see where you could declutter some of your health-related habits to further cleanse and clear and leave you open to receive!

Self-Assessment on Your Health

Are you struggling with your health at all?

Have you changed your eating habits at all in the past 10 years?

Do you exercise or move your body daily?

Do you find moving your body fun – by that I mean do you enjoy dancing, or going to a yoga class or taking long walks?

If you find exercise a chore, why is this? Explore this a little.

Does a takeaway meal feel like a luxury or is this part of life?

Are you shifting into a new stage of life (becoming a mother, moving into menopause)?

What would you class as a treat? Do you reward yourself with food?

Have you tried anything new regarding your health – giving up smoking, stopping booze for example?

Could you try something new regarding your health?

Health is wealth, and so whilst you may feel like I am nagging, it is as important to declutter our health habits as it is scrubbing the bathroom or emptying out the loft. And once again this isn't about overhauling your life, doing a diet and feeling miserable. It's about taking the small steps, decluttering a little here and there until you feel clearer and able to receive.

Major Life Events

This section isn't really a decluttering section as such, but major life events cause us to declutter, clear and let go in some way, so I wanted to mention them.

When we welcome new life into a family, there is a subtle shift that occurs in our relationships.

If you are the mother of an adult child who just gave birth – like me. In fact, whilst I was writing this book, we welcomed a new baby into our family.

There is a decluttering of the old relationship as we welcome in the new.

My girl is no longer my girl, she is now a mother to her own daughter. And I am not only a mother, I am a grandmother. We talked at length about the birth process. And while every fibre of my being wanted to be there while she gave birth – my mother's instinct kicking in, wanting to be there to take away the pain I knew my girl would be in – I also knew it was time for me to step back and give her and her husband the space to become their own unit. This involved a decluttering and reordering of how I think and approach my daughter. We are still in the early stages in this new chapter, but I have faith that we will muddle along just fine.

The same could be said with getting married, death, divorce and moving home. They say all these stages in life are the most stressful, but that is because they are rites of passage into a new chapter.

I also believe that these major life events do become stressful because we become fixed and fearful in our mindset, which in turn makes it hard to let go and move on to the next stage of this wonderful thing called life.

Seasons come and go. Every year we welcome in the spring, summer, autumn and winter. Death surrounds us in each season and cycle. Women, in particular, live this each month.

And death comes to us all – it is inevitable – and whilst it is painful to lose someone you love and care for, one thing I can share is, they are never truly gone.

Just around us in a different form.

Summary

If you have followed this section in a linear way (there is no right way...remember); my vacuum will be making its way through areas of your life; to come up and be healed or dealt with.

No more sweeping it under the carpet or hiding it at the back of a cupboard, where it cannot be seen. We have together opened up the windows and allowed the clarity to shine through.

I'd love to hear from you about your experiences that may have cropped up during the CLEARing phase of your journey.

Perhaps you have started to see correlations. Perhaps you just have a sparkling clean and clear living space. Perhaps you have realised you need to welcome in some new habits to bring back your sparkle. Or perhaps thanks to your self-assessments you are clear on what is really going on with that chap or lass down the road.

It's all good stuff. Really.

So are you ready... to Let Go?

L is for Letting Go

"Be like Elsa...
Let it go, let it go..."

Carolyn Creel

L is for Letting Go

"I can see clearly now the rain is gone
I can see all obstacles in my way
Gone are the dark clouds that had me blind
It's gonna be a bright (bright)
Bright (bright) sunshiny day."
Jimmy Cliff

This is often the hardest bit, and the bit that slows everyone down.

We will start to look at your life from a different perspective, and we will support you as you begin to Let Go of everything that could be weighing you down.

And I've already alluded to a lot of the areas that may feel difficult to Let Go in our CLEARing section.

If you have started to declutter your home for example and you now have a tonne of black bags sitting in your hallway, garage or boot – then well done, I applaud you for getting this far.

Letting Go of anything we have 'owned' or 'claimed' or that was ours IS hard. I wouldn't pretend otherwise. Letting Go brings with it a level of grief and hardship for us humans, especially if we have worked hard to attain it in the first place!

I am talking about all things here – not just clutter and stuff. Not just the wedding dress you have kept in the loft for 25 years or that old pram in the garage, which had all the memories of pushing your child around their first trip to Legoland. And don't get me started on the designer jeans you bought back in your 30s, which you have held onto because, not only did they cost a bomb, they represent a version of yourself you like to pop back and visit from time to time (you know, the one who had fun, once upon a time).

I am also talking about old habits – the saying *"Old habits die hard,"* – ne'er a truer word said, to my mind.

I am referencing relationships of old – you know the ones. The old school friends who you clung to on the first day of school. The next door neighbour you'd play with, out front in the summer. The university friends you roomed with. The women you went to mother and baby classes with.

I'll probably repeat myself a lot here – but there is always a reason, and a season for everything.

We just don't always want to part with it! And sometimes the Universe helps us out, and that's when it can become painful.

PS Leopards can for the record change their spots – they just have to be willing to put on a different coat.

Whilst writing this I saw something on social media which really struck me as true.

"Clutter is nothing more than postponed decisions," Barbara Hemphill.

It is also the physical, emotional and energetic baggage we have collected over the years.

You see, we can declutter, but if we don't Let Go of the emotional attachment that those 'things' – people, clothes, photos, objects – represent, then guess what? Nothing really changes.

Often, we don't realise just how much we needed to Let Go until we have released it.

I often use the analogy of gripping a pencil really hard. You have done it for so long that the way your hand feels – tight, clenched, and hanging onto that pencil for dear life – feels like normality. It's only when you loosen your grip you realise just how tightly you had held onto it. And your palm can be opened to receive.

We dive into this more later, but can you already sense how this works?

The more we hold onto things, whether it's worries, control, emotion, beliefs, we are stopping ourselves from receiving.

And as you have already found from beginning to clear your spaces, it's not the 'things' that matter. It's what they represent, energetically.

There is a real sense of freedom around Letting Go.

By starting to Let Go of belongings, we can lay the foundation for Letting Go of so much more.

The things that are keeping you stuck emotionally and energetically aren't always obvious.

If I sat you down right now, put the kettle on, and asked you to tell me all the emotions that are keeping you stuck, would you be able to do it?

I mean, I don't know about you, but I often don't realise that I am holding onto something so closely, so tightly, until I release it.

Just ask my best friend and business partner, Adam. He is so used to me ranting, going full on hairdryer treatment in his face, ranting until I feel it has all gone, then feeling so much better afterwards. Let's just say it's a good job he is my best friend and knows me well enough to not be caught off guard by my Linda Blair moments.

I often don't realise there is an Adam rant coming until I am in full throttle mode.

Maybe you can relate to that too?

It can so often be the tiniest things that set us off. Maybe your kids have left their cereal bowls on the side for the 4th day running after you have repeatedly asked everyone to please put their crockery in the dishwasher after meals. The next thing you know, you are in a full-on meltdown about no-one caring. You bring up all the other things that people do that seem inconsiderate, and it all seems to come from nowhere.

Of course it isn't from nowhere. You had been holding on tightly, and didn't realise you needed to Let Go.

If you have a tendency to feel this more, shall we say, acutely, before your cycle, you will know what I mean. Our hormones often accentuate things and help us to Let Go. The same with menopause; more on that later.

So what does this have to do with clearing your spaces?

Everything, actually.

As you shed your clutter in all your spaces, you will be continually Letting Go.

This can be some pretty challenging emotional work while you let feelings surface, some of which you may not realise had been buried for such a long time until they appear and take over every thought and emotion until you cry, shout, or scream it out.

Letting Go can be a really physical, visceral thing. Knowing how to move through these emotions is really key, and we look at more of the CLEAR Method dance space in the Energise section of this book. As you Let Go more and more, and find ways that work for you to move through all the feelings and emotions as they bubble up, the more you will discover what works for you.

It's worth noting here that feeling all the feels and Letting Go is NORMAL.

It can feel really uncomfortable, because we are trained and indoctrinated from an early age that showing our emotions isn't welcome, that we need to 'behave,' keep quiet, and not show our full range of feelings.

Of course, all this does is to make sure that we stuff our feelings right down inside, like the pair of socks you might find behind a drawer that you haven't emptied out for years.

You may not see it, but it's still there, still lurking, taking up space, and needing to be cleared.

And now all we are doing with the CLEAR Method is checking back in with all the things we have hidden away, and letting them go.

As we explore Letting Go of your belongings, you will notice that we meander through Letting Go of all kinds of things – endings, guilt, shame, worry, fear, outcomes, people, situations, expectations – you name it, it's all linked up.

More often than not, Letting Go of control is at the heart of it all; control around how we want things to be, hoped that they had been, or wish that we could change.

Letting Go is like a mini grieving process.

Every time you find yourself confronting a powerful emotion as you walk through the CLEAR Method, remember that this is powerful stuff, and go easy on yourself.

Find ways to nourish your nervous system (more on this in the Energise section), and please do take the time to celebrate doing this really important work.

Making changes in your own life has deep and lasting effects on the people around you, and it really does ripple out.

So yes, clearing out your sock drawer is a world changing act.

Believe me.

Letting Go Toolkit

Letting Go of the clutter can and will activate your emotions.

It's part of the process, and why the CLEAR Method is so much more than simply a list of things to clean or get rid of.

Having a toolkit to hand can really help you to move through the many feelings as they arise.

First of all, knowing where you are going to put this stuff can really help.

There are three potential ways you can help your clutter leave your spaces:

- Donations
- Dosh
- Dump

Donations

Let's start with donations.

Passing on clothes, toys, books and belongings can be a great way to bring abundance and joy to other people in need while also Letting Go of things you no longer need.

You might want to take your things to a charity shop, list them on Facebook Marketplace or Freecycle, or offer them to some local communities in need like refugees or community initiatives supporting families who need help.

A word of warning, though: Find the fastest, most efficient method that you can to get the stuff out of your house. I cannot emphasise this enough.

It's all too easy to bag something up for donation, then leave it in your attic, your garage, your hallway, or even your car boot for days, weeks, months even.

Guess what? You haven't Let Go if you do that. You have just moved the clutter and the energetic blockage somewhere else.

So find where to take your things, decide, and set aside time to do it.

Dosh

Next up, you could sell some of your things, and make some cash back on items you no longer need.

Listing on eBay, Facebook Marketplace, Vinted, or similar apps can be a great way to both Let Go of things and get some extra dosh while you do it.

The option definitely comes with a warning: if you choose to sell your items, set a time limit, on it, and if they don't sell, donate them or let them go another way.

It's so easy to end up with a stash of stock that becomes overwhelming, which becomes another clutter problem in itself.

My advice is that if you ARE going to sell some items, choose them carefully, make it as easy as possible on yourself, and make it fast.

Selling is also an option that can bring up more emotions as the Letting Go process becomes delayed.

When you have to photograph, list, and store your belongings before they sell, you add more layers to the act of Letting Go, and build in more opportunity to hold on.

So be warned! Be aware, and sell just a few items if you want to or need to. The rest, just donate if you can. The emotional attachment is far easier to manage.

Dump

Finally, dumping things.

This is a solution that can become so easily riddled with guilt. With all our awareness around recycling, reusing and the like, dumping things can feel so tricky.

So, use your discernment here, and donate or reuse as much as you can, but do NOT let yourself fall for the quagmire of guilt around dumping belongings.

If you don't get rid, your belongings will be clogging up your spaces and your energy. And it's a slippery road to guilt, hoarding, and your belongings owning you, not the other way around.

However you Let Go of your things, find a way to celebrate and to energise yourself as you do it.

Letting Go energetically is where the real work begins, though.

This is where you are most likely to give up and stash things back in your cupboards or attic, because you just can't Let Go of the family heirloom teaspoons, the letter your first boyfriend wrote to you, or your school textbooks.

All this means is that you have some more emotional and energetic Letting Go to do.

Here are some pointers that can form your Letting Go toolkit. You will find your own ways over time too, so add to this list as you go, and discover what works for you.

Mindful Releasing:

As you notice resistance to letting something go, check in with where you feel it in your body.

Which part of your body is feeling tight when you think about letting this item go?

Notice it, and be aware of any thoughts or emotions that arise for you.

Name them, and identify where they are in your body, in your energy, and say aloud the feeling.

See if you can also identify which version of you is having resistance, and help her to let it go.

You see, the past versions of us need healing, and moving through Letting Go allows them to be heard, healed, and witnessed.

For example, you find your old cot blanket that became a 'soother' as a child.

You notice that you feel sadness, nostalgia, and grief in your belly, your heart, and your throat.

Saying aloud, "I feel sadness, nostalgia, and grief in my belly, my heart and my throat," allows those feelings to be witnessed.

You check in, and realise it's your inner child of around 4 years old who is sad, because she was told she could not have this soother blanket any more, and had to 'grow up.'

So you could say, "I feel my inner 4 year old, and I see that she is sad."

Picture her in your mind. Bring her close to your heart.

What do you want to whisper to her?

Maybe she needs to feel that she can have something to soothe her still, or to know what she can use instead to feel safe.

Offer her an option that you can show her from your adult life.

Maybe you can show her your gravity weighted blanket, or a favourite pair of fluffy socks that can help her to feel safe now.

See if your past self wants to say anything else to you. Maybe a story springs to mind from childhood that you had forgotten about. Maybe you picture a scene and it twinges some emotion.

Going to your journal is a great place to witness what is coming through when you meet resistance to Letting Go.

Write it all down.

Thank your past self for showing you what she needed, and check back in with how you feel about Letting Go now.

How Grief CLEARs the Way to Connection

Grief is one of the most potent, powerful ways to CLEAR your way to connection, and is also a masterclass in Letting Go.

Now, it's not an easy route, by any means.

But it is one of life's inevitable experiences. And it certainly accelerates spiritual development and the channel to your psychic self.

Whether it's grieving a loved one, or moving through big changes in life such as divorce, kids leaving home, retirement, menopause, or any other significant shift, grief is powerful, physical, and rollercoaster ride that helps you to Let Go (eventually!).

At any given time in my life I have people all around me who are experiencing grief.

People often seem to think that I have had a lot of grief in my life and yes I have, to a certain extent, but no more than the next person.

I am someone who grieving people are drawn to. Maybe that's because I can sense spirit and I can reassure them that their loved ones are okay (they are, by the way).

I can bridge that gap for them, which helps grieving people to move through those super strong physical emotions that happen in the human body when we lose a loved one.

Grief is also one of the strongest ways to clear through your own connection, to your intuition, to source, your higher self.

It's such a strong emotion, which you will know if you've ever been through it.

The range of emotions that purge from your body are incredibly powerful – the rage, the fear, the guilt, the sadness, the frustration, the anger. These feelings and emotions are so viscerally strong that they really affect you in a physical way.

Often this manifests in the body too.

We tend to find when we are grieving that we have problems with the lungs, which is where in Chinese medicine, grief is stored.

You might find that your body becomes ill at certain times while you are grieving.

Maybe you'll just feel exhausted.

Many of us will have experienced this during and after the pandemic, while we were grieving either loved ones, or loss of our own freedom, loss of our old ways of life, shedding old identities.

As I've been writing this book, we experienced the death of the Queen, which highlighted the power of collective grief, a sense of shared loss that's amplified as the world shares in it in some way.

As grief moves through us, it clears the way for us to Let Go and Receive.

It's like the ultimate cleaning solution, the ultimate cleaning hack for our bodies, to help us connect to ourselves, to source, and of course, our psychic selves.

Grief is the most powerful emotional scourer that there is for your soul.

It's not an easy journey, but it is an extremely powerful emotion.

Grief really embodies the CLEAR Method. The sense of loss comes from clearing or decluttering people, identities, relationships, or situations.

Letting Go is where the work of grief is, and moving towards finding new energy – physically, emotionally, spiritually.

The actions we take during the grieving process, no matter how small, are the stepping stones to beginning to Receive what's waiting for us around the corner.

As I said before hanging onto things is like gripping a pencil in your hand for so long, and then if you let it go, what happens? The pencil drops, your hand relaxes, and you're able to Receive.

Grief takes us through that process of gripping so hard and resisting change to Receiving – and it's powerful stuff.

Ultimately, grief will always be with us. We are humans, after all.

It's about learning to live alongside it, to co-exist and move with grief, knowing that it has a powerful purpose to enrich our lives.

Journal Prompts:

Where have you experienced grief in your life?

How have those experiences helped you to receive more?

Where are you 'gripping the pencil' in life at the moment?

What are you afraid to Let Go of, because grief seems too much?

How can you shift that resistance, knowing that grief CLEAR's the way?

The Wedding Dress in the Cupboard

Ruth had kept her wedding dress in the cupboard for four years, although she never wore it to her wedding.

Her father had a stroke just a few weeks before the wedding day, and the event itself got postponed.

Not long after that, the pandemic took over, and many of the relatives and loved ones who would have been celebrating with Ruth, her partner and their family, had passed away.

The beautiful wedding dress remained in the cupboard, and she couldn't face opening the dress bag and deciding what to do with this gorgeous garment.

Of course, the issue was not the dress itself. Ruth needed to clear the clutter around that day, Let Go of the grief, and mourn the mountain of losses she still felt in her energy field. She needed to move through the sadness around the death of her family members, Let Go of the day that never was, and find a way to receive guidance on the next steps for their future. But for so long it felt overwhelming.

The dress became a symbol for the sadness yet to be processed, and the cupboard contained it, out of sight, away from awareness.

But of course the energy of the wedding and the un-CLEARed grief was bubbling away, and had been for the four years since she put the dress away.

For Ruth, healing was a cupboard door away.

As she found the courage to open the door, unpack her beautiful dress and grieve it all, she began to take steps to healing that pervasive sadness, and to open up a dialogue with her partner around this momentous day that they never shared.

Sacred Rage: How the Magic of Menopause Helps Us Let Go

The menopause is a really significant time in the life of a woman where the CLEAR Method comes into its own, naturally.

This is, of course, all about the shift from one stage of life to another, which can be rocky for some and not so much for others.

But either way, the way that our bodies, our hormones, and our identities naturally move into the next stage of life has a lot to do with the way that CLEAR Method works as well.

My Mum and my sister both really suffered with menopausal symptoms; hot flashes, the sweats, you name it. I used to look at them and think, "No thanks. I don't want any of that." And honestly, I don't suffer too badly.

I was really fortunate in that respect, but the perimenopause and in the time leading up to my menopause, I did struggle with lots of things. I felt anxious; I struggled to be social like I had been before. My brain wasn't working like it did. It was a really difficult, challenging time.

But when I reached menopause itself, I Let Go of that stage. And I cleared the way to this new phase of my life, in which I am receiving new guidance, new projects, and a whole new business, in actual fact. Since you're here reading this, you will know that to be true!

It reminds me that, just like grief, the menopause is almost like a portal to clear yourself. It is one of the most powerful ways, in order to receive your new identity, your new way of living, and to step into all that is coming to you in your second phase of life as a woman.

These days, there is much more awareness and discussion around menopause – I think for good and for bad.

I think it's great to have awareness for women and support available, as we navigate what can be a super challenging time. And I'm really pleased that these things are not taboo anymore.

But I do also think that we can spend too much time and energy sitting in the stories of how everything is so bad during menopause. We can label almost every symptom as menopausal, and once again, it's that collective fear, isn't it, that can be so easily clung on to? Just like I talk about gripping that pencil really hard. When we Let Go of it, we're able to Receive and our hands are open again.

Often we are gripping so hard onto stories and beliefs and other peoples' realities.

Not to say that you might not be suffering. Many people do, for many different reasons during this stage of life.

But let's keep in mind that we can stay in our own lane when it comes to experiencing menopause. Our story is our own story, our experience is our own experience, and to work within those parameters.

Whatever your perimenopause and menopause experience is, or has been, it is unique to you. It is your own. Almost like an initiation into the next powerful stage of being a woman. And one in which you Let Go of who you were before in your fertile years when you had your monthly bleed.

For me, I still experience symptoms and shifts at different points of my cycle even though I no longer have that cycle.

It's almost like our bodies are still linked to the moon and the seasons throughout a cycle in some way. It really is all quite magical, isn't it?

Knowing myself, being able to lean into what my body and soul needs at different times throughout the month, is still really important to me.

It's all about using your intuition to figure out what you need.

Sacred Rage

Sacred Rage has often been spoken about, especially more so recently. Rage is something that can really come through during the menopausal years, due to the fluctuating hormones and the way that we are experiencing such enormous peaks and troughs of oestrogen, progesterone and testosterone.

Emotions can really throw us, and sometimes the anger that needs to come out is expressed during this time.

Let me tell you, my rage was pretty potent in my perimenopause, and my mood swings were huge – as my daughter and my business partner will both tell you!

I'm much calmer now. But, I can really see that, with hindsight, sometimes those emotions needed to be decluttered and Let Go of, in order for me to receive what was coming next.

We should never fear the power of powerful emotions. Like grief – when I speak about how grief is almost like the CLEAR Method on steroids, and it's a natural way to process all these human emotions in our body – the menopause is the same.

Whenever we are feeling these amplified emotions, it's great to harness the energy of them; to use them to move through and to purge old habits or behaviours, knowing that as we move through this state we are stepping into one that is so much more open to receive, and so much more powerful.

Many women move through the menopause and feel so much more connected to themselves, connected to their psychic abilities and able to know themselves far more than they ever have before.

Journal prompts:

If you are experiencing heightened emotions during your perimenopause and menopause, what are they?

Have they helped you to move through some difficult situations in any way?

What are you Letting Go of in your identity as you move through into your next stage of life?

Who do you feel you are becoming?

How do you feel you are changing as a person as you shift into your older years as a woman?

How are you taking on other people's stories of menopause around you? Have they affected you and your own experience?

Are you able to Let any of them Go?

What would you love to receive at this stage in your life?

Summary

As I referenced at the beginning of this section, this can be the hardest bit of the CLEAR Method.

Letting Go and creating space, comes with a level of fear. Fear that when that person, or item has gone, what is left... ?

I mean, we've all seen what happens to a child when you force them to give up their blanky or dummy before they are ready... indeed there are tears and great resistance. But we know as adults that once they have stopped relying on their dummy, the feeling passes and it is like they never had it in the first place.

We are no different.

Which is why you can do this gradually.

There may be things you need to just store in the garage or in black bags ready to donate, dump or sell. There may be things, people or the past you need to make peace with and Let Go of. Bagging it up is the first step. Dumping it when ready is the next.

Just know once you have Let Go like Elsa, then comes freedom and space.

E is for Energise, Embody, Embrace and Empower

"The trick is not to
fill the space immediately."

Carolyn Creel

E is for Energise, Embody, Embrace and Empower

"Nobody can tell ya
There's only one song worth singing
They may try and sell ya
'Cause it hangs them up
To see someone like you
... But you gotta make your own kind of music
Sing your own special song
Make your own kind of music
Even if nobody else sings along."
-     *'Make Your Own Kind Of Music'* Cass Elliot

Welcome to the Energise section of the CLEAR Method.

Energising is such a core part of the CLEAR Method dance.

You see, really this is all about shifting energy; whether we are Clearing, Letting Go or Receiving, Energising is really all about helping that process along, and noticing how the energy is changing in your life in certain situations, conversations, relationships, and environments.

You might notice as you go through the CLEAR Method, that your energy is naturally shifting, and that the way you think about certain people, things, places, and situations changes, that your physical energy has shifted.

In this chapter, we're going to be looking at different ways that you can help to shift energy, depending on what you need.

You can use some tools in the CLEAR Method toolkit to Energise whatever situation you are navigating at any point in time.

Far from being all about movement, Energising can also be resting, speaking aloud what you need, having a good old rant (just ask Adam, my business partner about my infamous hairdryer treatment!), reading a book, or even watching absolute trash on TV (my go-to for winding down my brain).

When you Let Go of your clutter, it immediately creates a space for a fresh new energy that will Energise you.

The trick and difficulty is not to fill that space straight away.

We have been taught from a young age to fill time; scheduled break time in amongst all our scheduled learning. Then when we move into adulthood and make an honest crust, we continue to fill our time – with meetings for meetings sake, creating processes and clutter.

For those of us who work 9 to 5 there are surely times of the day where we could literally sit and do nothing. But it is programmed into us to fill that time because we are effectively on the clock.

This is something I wanted to address when Adam and I set up the company. We wanted to empower our team to work more effectively. So we took the decision to finish our working day an hour earlier. Our teams work 9 to 4.30 and we have never been more effective or efficient. The extra hour a day means our employees can take time for themselves however that works for them.

So hopefully you are now at that part of your journey where you have let some of the clutter go.

Whether it's physical or emotional; you should feel 'emptier' or 'clearer.'

It is completely normal to want to fill this lovely clean space almost immediately.

I mean, have you ever decluttered your drawers of old clothes, only to rush out and purchase a whole new wardrobe?

My advice to you here is simple.

Consciously stop and do nothing. Just be in the space. Press pause.

If you have decluttered space in your day; why not block out the empty space and sit and enjoy it. Take time to enjoy a cup of tea under a soft blanket.

Embrace the space, and empower yourself through enjoying a clear fresh front room, or an empty diary so you can take time out doing something you love.

Try not to fill it up with more clutter and think about what Energises you and how can you invite more of that into your life?

Feeling the Energetic Shifts of CLEARing

If you have ever started a fitness or wellbeing health kick, you know that you begin to feel immediate effects by looking after yourself.

Within a couple of weeks, you feel so much better within yourself. Within about a month, your whole energy has shifted and people are commenting on your visible change.

It's a little bit like that with the CLEAR Method.

You see, when you start making those tiny changes at home just by taking a few minutes to empty out a drawer, or to make a pile to Let go of, or to declutter your digital space, the change is almost imperceptible at first. But, each tiny tweak that you make has a significant impact on your overall energy and on the progress that you're making, to not only connect to your higher self, but to clear the environment around you.

It's that magic of the compound effect, isn't it? Lots and lots of tiny changes really quickly add up. And I promise you, before long you will be really feeling those shifts in your energy.

This was certainly the case for Jeanne. She came from a house that was incredibly cluttered as a child, and in her mid-life was supporting her elderly Mum with a house that was completely crumbling.

This was really draining on her energy. And also wasn't giving her much time to clear and stay on top of her own house. But she knew only too well the pitfalls of not clearing things out, after all the evidence was there in front of her every time she saw her Mum.

So, as overwhelmed as she was, she just began by setting a timer for 10 or 15 minutes each day, and decluttering a tiny area in her home.

Within just a couple of weeks, the spaces around her began to feel much cleaner, much clearer, and way, way easier to keep on top of.

Her home felt like a lovely, clear space to be, rather than a muddled, messy, confusing place that contributed to the overwhelm she was constantly muddling through.

She also found, much to her surprise, that as she cleaned, she found the space in her thoughts to process emotions, and to connect to herself. In fact, it became almost like a meditation.

Maybe you will find that too. Even if you have really been someone in the past who has disliked cleaning or clearing, that time really is something that's personal. There's such a ritual in taking just a few minutes to clear your space.

Jeanne began to really look forward to her decluttering times in the day, and she put them in her diary as an appointment with herself.

She put on some music, discovered some cleaning products that she really enjoyed using, and before long the whole family were also helping to keep the spaces clean and clear.

Before, they'd muddled through a family home that was fairly chaotic, although not unusual. Cleaning was something that happened once a week, and felt quite overwhelming and time-consuming for Jeanne, with all the things that she was juggling.

Now it became something that was part of a daily routine. Items were becoming cleared out regularly, and much to her surprise, her own physical energy began to really improve, as did her connection to intuition.

It was a huge surprise to her just how quickly this stuff worked.

Maybe you'll feel that surprise too, as you move through the tools here.

You might even notice it much faster than Jeanne. Or maybe you won't notice – then one day there you are working on a little area of your house with joy, just realising how much this lifts you up.

The energy of the CLEAR Method is the part that often surprises people.

The way in which we feel so energised when our spaces become clearer really is incredible – it's like an outward detox! If you've ever felt the effects of eating in a really healthy way for a long period of time, when your mind is clear, you feel more energised, you're able to face the day.

That's how it is when you work with all of your spaces – your physical, mental, emotional, spiritual and energetic spaces.

Calling Back Your Energy Ritual

So during the course of writing this book, I spent some time with my creative team; and one thing we found after we had gone through the decluttering and clearing process in my own business (yes I do actually apply the CLEAR Method in everything I do); I felt a little discombobulated, and then I was reminded by Spirit that I needed to call back my scattered self.

Nothing deep, like a soul retrieval – though I've had one of those and they are quite painful but amazing.... it's more about calling those parts of yourself you left in other people's fields.

I liken it to when you go round the house picking up all the socks, jumpers, handbags, paperwork and half-drunk cups of tea, when you are straightening your space out.

If you have strewn physical parts of yourself all over the home, imagine what you are doing with your energy.

I know you can't see it, but you can feel it when you are scattered. It normally comes with a huge sense of overwhelm and stuckness.

I actually find myself doing this every day. It's just good hygiene isn't it!

And, I was guided to share this with my team after our session. One of them was expressing deep overwhelm. I could clearly see she needed to call back those parts of herself into wholeness and have her body fully embody her again, so she could think clearly and be present.

We (especially women) have been sold the lie that we can multitask/spin all the plates.

Well we can, and we do. In fact, I am a great believer that you can have it all. You just need to learn the tools on how to best navigate that, so you're not the one who loses out.

But when we are multi-tasking ourselves and often others around us, we can drop fragments of our energy, meaning we are the ones who are energetically drained.

We forget to take the time out to create a pause or a vacuum.

Again, I want to tell you that you cannot do any of this wrong. It is just a case of making small and tiny changes to enhance your life.

But perhaps try this, each morning before you get up and into the throes of life, take five minutes to assess your energetic field.

Take some cleansing deep breaths, and scan your body from your feet right through to your head.

See if you can sense any holes or invisible chords.

Often I get images in my mind when I find a chord – normally relating to a person or an activity.

I invite you to gently call that chord back and send love to that person or space that chord had been attached to.

Or another way I like to do this, is to imagine I am a jigsaw puzzle and those pieces that are missing are hiding under the sofa in that meeting from yesterday; or in the car with my daughter; or out shopping with friends.

I go searching for the jigsaw pieces and complete the puzzle that is me.

Then once complete, I imagine a bubble of protection or a cling film cover that gently protects and prevents my energetic puzzle from falling apart.

Both of these suggestions are great when you are feeling overwhelmed or scattered.

And of course, physically clearing the space of odd socks is a great help too.

One thing about this segment of the book, is to try to fill up your cup.

Energise and embody all the CLEAR space in your home and in your mind.

Taking regular space to pause will Energise you!

And if you still really struggle, something I love to do and cannot recommend enough is to read a book (not a TV show, though that sometimes is a good solution). A book is perfect because you are having to read and therefore focusing on the words, not the issues that could be plaguing you.

I prefer fiction in this case and if you have a Kindle Unlimited subscription like me you can find yourself devouring books quite regularly.

I have even set up a playlist in Spotify for you to sit with your cup of PG Tips, so go have a listen; or read the damn book!

How to Energise Your CLEARing

There will likely be many times in your CLEARing process, as you go through the cycle, that you will need to shift through blocks, maybe process some emotions, move through resistance, or indeed to celebrate all the magic that's happening in your life.

Having a range of tools in your toolkit that you can use can be really useful to have to hand.

The way that we move through energy will be different for each of us. And I invite you to explore and to play with what feels good, so that you can discover what works for you.

First of all, let's just take a look at why – why do we need to shift energy?

Can energy really get stuck?

Well, actually, yes. Often this is why our bodies create disease, or injuries, or illness.

As woo as it sounds, it's simply energy being stuck in one place.

Moving through feelings, emotions and experiences really helps our human bodies, the human experience of our souls here on earth, to release some of that energy.

Remember, emotions are just energy in motion. Learning to move them through is a powerful tool in your CLEAR Method box of tricks.

For example, you might be feeling really sluggish or tired, and maybe your body is needing to rejuvenate and find some extra zing.

A go-to thing for you might be to put on some tunes, and to really just shake it out – activate the Chi energy in your body, build the tingles in your arms, your toes, your feet.

Maybe you are feeling anxious. So what you need to do is to find some calm through breathwork or meditation or some yoga poses.

A yin yoga practice from YouTube can be great. Or as I mentioned earlier, pick up a book to calm and soothe your monkey mind.

Identifying which emotions are present, and how you can free them up, is such a powerful piece of your CLEAR Method toolkit.

Let's look at just some of the techniques that can help you to move emotions and to shift them from your body, to move them around.

Breathwork
Let's start with breathwork.

Breathwork is perhaps one of the most easily accessible tools to use, because it requires nothing other than just you and your breath, which last time I checked, comes with us everywhere we go.

There are many different ways to use the breath to shift energy, to change it, and to move through it. I like to use a few different practitioners who have created some brilliant videos on YouTube; just search 'breathwork' and you will see what I mean.

For example, you might want to look at box breathing, a 5-7-8 breathing technique, or maybe even breath holds. Each type of breathwork has a different effect on your body, and can actually change the physical state of your body and your energetic field. Amazing, isn't it, what the breath can do?

Even just by taking 5, 10, or 15 minutes from your day, you can shift your body from anxious to calm, and from stressed to serene, or from agitated to aligned.

So, take a look, experiment with some things that work for you and come back to them.

Yoga is always a brilliant tool to help move through energy. Now, I'm not a massive fan of yoga poses myself, I far prefer a dog walk in nature to shift my energy, but you might like to try it and see how it resonates.

Again, there are many resources online for free that you can use to find a practice that works for the amount of time that you have and for the feeling or emotion that you are present to and working with.

Exercise

Yoga is such an ancient tradition and practice, with 1000s of years and a wealth of experience around how the body, the meridians and the breath align to create harmony and balance.

If it works for you, then definitely include this in your exercise toolkit.

Sometimes you just need to go and hit the pavement in your trainers, or go to the gym with some weights.

Again, that's not my favourite way of doing it – I love to walk the dogs – but maybe you love a good Zumba session or you really love to go and shake it all out in a dance class.

Find a way to exercise that can help teach your body to let go of excess energy to get your heart pumping, your blood racing.

Maybe you might want to play and experiment with different forms of exercise.

If you don't already have a routine, this can be really fun.

Making it part of your routine can really help you to allow your energetic field to process all the things you are Clearing and Letting Go of, to enable you to Receive and Activate.

Singing and Speaking Aloud

Singing is such an important part of energetic work that can be so often overlooked.

Singing actually activates and stimulates the vagus nerve. It allows the whole body to vibrate and shifts your energetic field.

There's a reason why people in choirs often say that it's so good for their wellbeing. Obviously, being part of a community is a huge piece of that, but also the way that sound vibrates throughout your bones, your muscles, and your body is so powerful. Plus, you're using your throat chakra to create noise which can really help to clear aggression.

So whether you are putting on the tunes loud at home and singing along or you are part of a choir, see if singing is a way that can release or move through energy for you.

Speaking aloud what we want to call in, or what we are feeling, is so powerful too.

Women in particular have been trained to not ask for what we want, and by using our voices to ask aloud for support, to name what we feel, or to let out emotions is an incredibly potent thing to do. Even if no-one is listening (but of course, they are – your guides are always with you).

Dance
Dancing is one that I absolutely love, and it's one of my favourite ways to move through energy.

There are so many different types of dance, but just moving your body to music is the basis of it, and that can look like however it needs to look for you. (Let me tell you, it doesn't look glamorous for me, but I love it!)

Maybe you love the Five Rhythms dancing. Maybe you'd love to put the drum and bass on, turn it up loud and let your body move. Maybe you are far more of a Strictly Come Dancing, cha-cha-cha or waltz fan.

Whatever it is, moving your body with rhythm and flow is an incredible way to move through energy and emotions.

Music always works for me, and I love to put on my music really, really loud.

I open the windows at home and just dance it out as if no-one's watching. They probably are, but let's pretend they're not, eh?

Rest

Resting and taking time to just 'be' is a part of energising that can be so easily overlooked.

Resting – intentional, calm, nourishing rest – is sometimes exactly what you need.

We often talk about moving energy around, and dance, music, exercise, are all amazing ways to do that, but being still and allowing things to integrate is also incredibly powerful.

You might feel the need to sit and meditate, or just take a few moments to breathe deeply and just observe your body, your mind, your breath.

Resting is energising too. We need to let go of the old beliefs that you can't sit being idle. Who the heck decided that was a good idea?

The Italian phrase Dolce la far niente is all about the concept of the joy of doing nothing; whether that's going for a walk, spending time reading a book on your sofa, or watching a movie in the middle of the afternoon.

Oh, and the key part of that? It's Letting Go of the guilt that comes alongside doing nothing.

Yep. If you imagine, right now, taking an hour to yourself doing exactly what you want to do, notice what pops into your head.

Is it the washing up that needs to be done? The kids' uniforms that need washing? The cat's vet appointment that needs scheduling? The sticky floor that needs a clean? Your shopping list, or planning what to eat later?

Listen, leaning into doing nothing is hard. We have been trained by society for our whole lives to be DO-ing.

BE-ing is a whole new skill set to learn, and it takes time. Be kind to yourself.

Being mindful of what feels supportive in the way you energise your body and your energetic field is an intuitive tool that will deepen over time.

Energising Your Environment
Energising your environment is a really interesting way to change the energy of a place.

We've looked at energising you and your body, and changing the energy in our environment is something that's really important too.

A number of things you might like to try include:

- Opening your windows and doors to let in fresh air;

- Sounding some singing bowls around the house to shift some vibrations;

- Including crystals in your environment. Some of my favourites are Rose Quartz, Amethyst, Clear Quartz, Selenite and Moonstones, all of which clear and bring gentle vibes to a room.

- Using colour to change the energy of a room – by adding a throw, some new paint, some artwork, or lighting.

Building Your Own Energise Toolkit

Take a moment to jot down some possible ways to energise your body and your environment.

This way, when it comes to shifting through energy and emotion, you already have a mini toolkit to hand that you can call upon.

When I feel sad I could:

When I feel angry, I could:

When I feel sluggish, I could:

When I feel excited, I could:

When I feel overwhelmed, I could:

Energising things that I haven't tried yet but would like to:

You will find as you continue on your CLEAR journey that new ways to move through energy and emotion will find their way into your life, as you meet new people, discover new practices, and deepen your spiritual awareness.

Make a note of them as they arrive, and try whatever feels like it could be fun or aligned with you.

If it feels good, add them to your toolkit, and build your own bespoke Energise toolkit as you grow and evolve.

I would love to hear what's working for you. Let me know by tagging me on Instagram @carolynspiritual, or send me an email carolyn@carolyncreel.com

Energise Assessment and Toolkit

Take a moment and go within, sit with yourself, and take a few deep breaths.

Scan your physical body first by placing your attention on each part of your body in turn.

Stay present to where you feel tightness – perhaps hunched shoulders, tight muscles, a sense of clenching, pain, heat, or cold. There is no right or wrong, just notice what is.

Now do the same with your energetic field. You don't need to worry about how to find it, just imagine the space around you as a ball of light, and see if you can sense anything in the energetic vicinity around you.

Now, this might seem crazy at first. And I hear you. But the more you clear, the more you check in with yourself, and the more time you spend tuning in, the easier and more natural this will seem.

As you start with this practice, it can be helpful to write down what you notice, so you can check in with yourself and see what changes after you use the toolkit.

So ask yourself:

What am I feeling right now?

What can I do to shift it?

See if you can identify what feels good to you to Energise those feelings from the toolkit.

As you begin to get used to this, you might identify something like this:

I can feel a headache, my shoulders are hunched, and I have been holding my breath. I can identify sadness, grief, and anger.

To move through these, I want to speak aloud my feelings, dance around to my favourite song, then enjoy some quiet time with a cuppa, a candle, and my book.

Trust that you know what you need. Because you do, by the way

Now, use one of the Energise tools in your toolkit.

You might even want to piggyback a few.

Check back in with yourself:
What has changed?

What feels different?

How has that energy shifted?

What did you learn about doing this?

Now, the more you stop and notice what you need, and take a moment to move through it, running through this sequence of questions in your head becomes second nature.

Summary

Hopefully you have learnt in this section, the more you pause, stop and re-energise yourself, the easier it becomes. My golden rule for E of the CLEAR Method is to Energise yourself WITHOUT filling the holes left from Decluttering and Letting Go.

Sitting in the space you have created. Enjoying the space you have cleared.

It will get to the point, you won't need to write it down or journal each time you check in, it will become simply part of your self-awareness and self-care practice, and like second nature.

You will also begin to notice when you are stepping into sabotage and giving yourself the opposite of what you need a common thing, by the way, so don't feel bad about it, just begin to be aware of it.

Building deep trust in yourself and knowing how to give yourself what you need starts with the baby steps of checking in, trusting what you feel and perceive, and taking action to Energise. Over time you will develop a deep liking of who you are, loving yourself and supporting yourself with what you need.

This is a radical act in a society where putting our own needs anywhere near the top of the list is still considered inherently selfish.

On the other hand, when we begin to look after ourselves and what we need, little by little the world changes – one dance move, one loud rant, one sofa afternoon at a time. By taking the smallest steps to Clear and Energise, we can turn spiralling emotions and feelings from plummeting down into the doldrums to meandering their way back up to the dance floor.

So many people never learn to do this, and to take responsibility for their emotions.

So well done.

The fact you have this in your hands means you are already taking huge steps to CLEAR-ly see what you need and how to give it to yourself.

Let's put the kettle on for a brew and celebrate.

Oh, a glass of wine, did you say?

Go on, then...

A is for Action, Assessment and Alignment

"Pick your favourite bits,
and do more of that!"

Carolyn Creel

A is for Action, Assessment and Alignment

"Midnight, moonlight
The wind blows off Saint Clair."
Above and Beyond

This section does exactly what it says on the tin!

You will probably have noticed throughout this book there are regular spaces to assess where you are in the process. And I mentioned at the very beginning, CLEARing is like a dance, where all spaces are connected to each other.

This section is your self-assessment, taking action and getting into complete alignment dance space.

This will continuously come up as we work together.

You may have decluttered your home; and there are piles of bags in the boot of your car, in the 'holding' space until you are ready to 'take action.'

By this point, I would suggest things are a little clearer in your mind, so you can start to take action with no attachment.

Attachment to things and people is actually a big part of this process.

When we release attachment to the past, our past relationships, the way we always did things and how we behaved; we are able to welcome in the new.

It is that Act of Letting Go; which enables us to take action without the bags of guilt, shame and fear we so often carry around with us.

It's also the simple changes and acts that make a big difference. In my case, when I set up my business 20 years ago, I had worked for major corporate cleaning companies who metaphorically kept layering on the polish (Ladies, polish on polish... imagine the layers and layers).

So buying in more cleaning products, adding new forms to process, building more and more 'clutter' in; but with no-one appearing to take ownership to remove what didn't work anymore. I learnt from all of this, and when I began my cleaning company, my partner Adam and I decided to take what resonated and leave the rest.

We started with three basic cleaning products (bathroom, kitchen and floor cleaners). We had two forms (one time we were filling in an AR form on site, wondering what it was we were filling in... it was only a bloody Air Raid form back from the 40s!)

This section will help you to strip back to the basics, and help you to keep things simple, moving forwards so you can take what resonates in your life and leave the rest.

It is my intention that by taking action and regularly assessing your life, will change the way you think, the way you look at life, and to follow through with removing the clutter that is needed to create energetic, physical, mental and emotional space.

And so it begins...

CLEAR Method Audit

Make notes under each of these sections, and help yourself to orientate where you are right now as you begin your CLEAR Method adventure.

You could use a journal to do this, or answer right here in the book, whatever feels the most supportive for you right now.

Question 1:

As I begin my CLEAR Method journey I am most looking for clarity on:

Question 2:

The most challenging situation in my life right now is:

Question 3:

I would love to feel clearer in the following areas:

Question 4:

Who is the person I am becoming? How will I know when I am feeling progress?

Morning CLEAR Ritual

This five minute ritual can be done daily to help keep you on track and your mind clear.

Keep a journal or notepad by your bed; and each morning before you start anything, journal on the following questions:

- Clear – What is my intention and focus for the day?
- Let Go – What do I need to let slide/or Let Go of today?
- Energise – How can I energise myself today? What lights me up?
- Action – What three things need actioning today?
- Receive – What would I like to receive today?

This is a great way to plug any leaky energy gaps and see you right.

Quick Daily Actions for CLEARing Your Space

Home
Remember these jobs can be taken by any family member. And when your children are old enough, give them responsibility for keeping their own spaces CLEAR.

Kitchen
- Wash all dirty dishes, pots and pans or empty dishwasher
- Wipe down all surfaces with kitchen cleaner

- Tidy stray items away
- Do a quick vacuum and mop round.

Lounge
- Open windows first thing
- Tidy stray items away
- Wipe down surfaces with microfibre cloth
- Vacuum the carpet or rugs
- Plump up cushions.

Bathroom
- Hang up towels and open windows
- Change loo roll if needed
- Wipe round sink and bath / shower with a bathroom cleaner
- Use toilet brush in loo and drop some bleach in
- Remove any dirty clothes or stray items.

Bedrooms
- Make the beds or turn them down to allow fresh air
- Plump pillows
- Open windows
- Tidy stray items away and hang up clothes
- Wipe round surfaces with a microfibre cloth

Hallway
- Put shoes away or tidy the area
- Pick up post, recycle leaflets and deal with letters when they arrive
- Hang up coats
- Vacuum welcome mat.

Fridge

- Once a week, go through fridge, remove and bin anything past its use by date
- Wipe round with microfibre cloth and soapy water.

Quick Daily Action Lists for CLEARing

Self and Energy

Energy Clearing Action List

- Write down three things you would like to achieve that day
- Meditate for 15 mins
- When you shower, imagine it washing away anything that is no longer serving you
- Imagine a protective bubble of energy to prevent any negative energy cluttering your space
- Then before bed repeat the same – clear your bubble and imagine negative thoughts going down the plug hole.

Five Minute Energetic Self-Assessment Ritual – Calling all parts back

Take some cleansing deep breaths, and scan your body from your feet right through to your head.

See if you can sense any holes or invisible chords.

Often, I get images in my mind when I find a chord – normally relating to a person or an activity.

I invite you to gently call that chord back and send love to that person or space that chord had been attached to.

Or another way –

I imagine I am a jigsaw puzzle and there are pieces that are missing.

Perhaps they are hiding under the sofa in that meeting from yesterday; or in the car with my daughter; or out shopping with friends.

I go searching for the jigsaw pieces and complete the puzzle that is me.

Then once complete, I imagine a bubble of protection or a cling film cover that gently protects and prevents my energetic puzzle from falling apart.

CLEAR Self-Assessment – Family

This is a more in-depth assessment you can do when it comes to family and relationships.

See these as a quick reference guide when things are getting stuck. If you are needing help figuring out why something is clunky or stuck, revisit these questions. They may help you to figure out what action you need to take. We are cyclical beings, so one thing is for certain, nothing stays the same, and the answers to these questions will change as you move through life.

1. Think about your close family relationships to see where you (or they) could be stuck in the past. Who comes to the forefront of your mind when you ponder on this? How are you feeling right now?

2. When you look at your child, do you still see them as an infant? By that I mean, do you still baby your child, do things for them they perhaps can do themselves? How are you feeling at this moment?

3. When you look at your siblings, do you find yourself revisiting a time when you were younger? When your sister stole your favourite shoes and returned them damaged? Or your brother used to pick on you in front of his friends. How are you feeling at this moment?

4. When you look at your parents, what memories come up for you? Are they still perhaps treating you like a young adult? How do you feel about that relationship now?

Often these stuck records occur when you are shifting into new phases of life – when you give birth, when you leave school or college, or your child moves into being more independent.

And often these thoughts and glitches in our family relationships just need to be recognised, Cleared and Let Go of.

Self-Assessment –
Friendships and Connections

- Do you feel stuck with some of your friendships?

- Are there friends in your life who you haven't heard from in over a year?

- Do you feel invisible to some friends?

- Do you do all the running in some friendships?

- Are you clinging onto friendships from school or college just because you feel you should?

- What are your Social Media channels like? Are you collecting old friends or do you regularly cull those you no longer see in real life?

- Speaking about Facebook and other social media for a minute, when you post, does it feel uncomfortable? Are you worried certain people will see what you are sharing, because of what they will think? If so, are they truly your friends now? Little suggestion, these are probably the people you should mute or unfriend.

- Do you check up on old friends – or lurk in the past? Perhaps ask yourself why you are doing that – what needs to be decluttered so you can move into clarity?

Self-Assessment on Love

These questions are a little more specific to those people looking for love.

- Are you having a hard time holding a relationship down?

- Do you find it hard to attract love?

- What traits would you wish to see in an ideal partner?

- Are you looking for love or lust?

- What do you want from a partner?

- Do you check up on old loves on Facebook and other social media – do you find it hard to get closure?

- How do you feel about yourself?

Often when we are struggling to attract our life partner it is because we need to declutter our own thoughts about ourselves. To truly attract someone who is aligned with you, it starts with making sure you know who you are, and you love who you are.

Self-Assessment on Business or Job

- How is your work situation right now?

- Are you generally happy with the work you do?

- Do you enjoy the work?

- Is there anything you don't enjoy doing?

- Where can you clear out any unnecessary clutter in your business, or job?

- And to take this a step further, do you have a crowded desk or mailbox? Are you cluttering up your emails with old emails from two years ago?

- Are you on top of where your money is going? Do you know what your money is spent on?

- Are you spending money on old memberships you no longer need?

- Can you review contracts with mortgages, energy providers to make them go further for you?

- Is there anything you decluttered from the home that can be sold on to add more fluidity to your cash flow?

Money and our career is also connected to our Root Chakra. When this is functioning as it should then you will have more than enough money to keep a roof over your head and your basic human needs.

Self-Assessment on Your Health

- Are you struggling with your health at all?

- Have you changed your eating habits at all in the past 10 years?

- Do you exercise or move your body daily?

- Do you find moving your body fun – by that I mean do you enjoy dancing, or going to a yoga class or taking long walks?

- If you find exercise a chore, why is this? Explore this a little.

- Does a takeaway feel like a luxury or is this part of life?

- Are you shifting into a new stage of life (becoming a mother, moving into menopause)?

- What would you class as a treat? Do you reward yourself with food?

- Have you tried anything new regarding your health – giving up smoking, stopping booze for example?

- Could you try something new regarding your health?

Health is wealth, and so whilst you may feel like I am nagging, it is as important to declutter our health habits as it is scrubbing the bathroom or emptying out the loft. And once again this isn't about overhauling your life, doing a diet and feeling miserable. It's about taking the small steps, decluttering a little here and there until you feel clearer and able to receive.

Action List for Every Three Months – Seasonal self-assessments

Spring (March - May)

- Spring cleaning – now is traditionally the time we do a deep clean
- Clean your windows, move sofas and furniture to vacuum behind
- Declutter a room or space
- Set a new intention for the next three months
- Plant some seeds
- Make sure life admin is taken care of
- Check in with all your relationships – tune in and see who is in your field
- Social Media cull – remove yourself from groups you are not active in
- Plug any energetic leaks
- Tie up any loose ends
- Put your cosmic order in
- Review how far you've come.

Summer (June - August)

- Typically the weather is getting better, so it's perfect to have the windows and doors open to welcome in new energy
- Clean your windows, move sofas and furniture to vacuum behind
- Check in with your intention from Spring
- Nurture your seeds
- Declutter a room or space
- Spend time in nature – cloud gazing is a great activity to energise yourself

- Make sure life admin is taken care of
- Check in with all your relationships – tune in and see who is in your field
- Social Media cull
- Put your cosmic order in
- Review how far you've come.

Autumn (September - November)

- Harvest time
- Clean your windows, move sofas and furniture to vacuum behind
- Declutter a room or space
- Make sure life admin is taken care of
- Check in with all your relationships - tune in and see who is in your field
- Social Media cull
- Put your cosmic order in
- Review how far you've come.

Winter (December - February)

- Winter Solstice brings the shortest days – now is traditionally the time we do a deep clean
- Clean your windows, move sofas and furniture to vacuum behind
- Declutter a room or space
- Make sure life admin is taken care of
- Check in with all your relationships – tune in and see who is in your field
- Social Media cull
- Put your cosmic order in
- Review how far you've come.

Cosmic Ordering or Manifestation

One thing woo folk bang on about is manifesting. You'll hopefully have realised that manifesting the life you want, does require a little balance, meaning...

Conscious clear action taking AND manifesting or having clear goals.

I mean I didn't just meditate every day and boom became a successful business owner.

That took 20 years of listening to my intuition, taking action, asking for help and manifesting all in collaboration with Spirit.

But being clear means you can double down on the manifesting or cosmic ordering. Each quarter or moon cycle or significant energetic portal, I like to journal on what I'd love to manifest in my life.

I normally focus on a few things, but my suggestion to you as part of taking action is to list what you'd like to manifest into your life.

It could be a new car, a new home.

It could be more money.

It could be that your family is happy and healthy.

Listing this out can help you to clearly see (when you reflect back as you buy your shiny new car) all the steps you've taken along the way to enable you to reach that point.

Gratitude List

This is a favourite of mine, and so many neuroscientists and psychologists will support me when I say this is a great daily practice to help rewrite old thoughts and programmes and declutter old ways of doing things.

It's a great thing to do on a Friday afternoon or when you are feeling low.

Prompts include:
- What gifts have you received lately?
- Who are you grateful for this week?
- What are you grateful for this week?
- Have you asked for help? Did you receive it?

Take time out to really notice when the Universe has rewarded you or answered your cosmic order.

Summary

This section is the 'bossy' bit of this book. In fact I nicknamed her the 'Bossy Book' when I started writing it. I wanted to condense some of the 'taking action' parts into a space where you can dive into as and when you need to.

Because once we have Cleared, Let Go, taken Action, re-Energised and Aligned ourselves, we are so much more clear and open to Receive the gifts that the Universe has to offer.

A tidy house is the sign of a tidy mind. One that is ready to Receive. And so here we are the last section of the Bossy Book.

Now pay attention – this is the hardest one of all. Because for the most part, none of us are very good at Receiving.

Let's change that shall we?

Well what are you waiting for? Grab a cuppa and settle down in your nice sparkly home and enjoy.

R is for Receive

R is for Receive

Once you have Cleared the way,
then the final step is to Receive.

Making space to Receive all the goodness
that will undoubtedly flow your way.

Now we come to the last part of The CLEAR Method, and it's all about Receiving.

What is Receiving?

Often when we think of receiving, wealth is the first thing that comes to mind; we might think about winning the lottery, a sudden windfall, or increasing our income, but it's not always about money.

In fact, far from it.

Receiving translates to every single area of our lives. We can Receive thanks and praise, support and encouragement. We can Receive gifts, we can Receive space, we can Receive all sorts of amazing things.

In fact, if you are blocked from Receiving in one area, it's pretty much a given that you are blocked in others.

Now that you've been clearing up your home, your environment, your physical space, your mental space, and your energetic space, this is where you can really start to put your attention on receiving.

Re-Learning to Receive

Our ability to receive can be affected by so many things.

Old beliefs, habits, or stories that have been passed down from generations above us can really clutter up our ability to Receive.

Different generations and different cultures might have various expectations and tacit assumptions about what Receiving looks like - whether it's around roles in the home, how compliments are given, or how much money we could or 'should' earn.

Or, maybe it's something that was instilled in us in childhood about being able to Receive, be it money, love, support, praise, or anything else.

In fact, Receiving can be quite the minefield!

But the good news is that doing the energetic work of Clearing, Letting Go, Activating and Energising, really sets the stage for calling in more in your life.

Your ability to Receive is often highlighted in everyday encounters, perhaps without you realising it.

If you have ever been complimented on your outfit, for example, and come straight back with the, "This old thing? Ah, I got it on sale and just threw it on today," or a similar deflection, you will know *exactly* what I am talking about.

Somewhere in your brain, you have become wired to not accept that compliment, or to feel awkward about saying, simply, "Thank you! I really like it too."

Maybe your friend offers to buy a coffee for you, and you immediately waive your purse around in a frantic effort to beat them to it – "No no no, *I'll* get this!"

Or, at work your manager compliments you on a job well done.

If every piece of your being feels embarrassed about accepting the praise and being perceived as big-headed, conceited, or above yourself, there are still more things to Clear and Let Go before you can activate and practise owning being in Receiving mode.

Have you started to recognise yourself in any of these yet?

The energy of pushing things away becomes so obvious once you become aware of it. In fact, clients often tell me they feel themselves cringe when they are aware of pushing something away.

Awareness is a great place to start, and re-learning to Receive is like training a muscle – you become stronger at it over time.

Often, we have to literally re-learn to receive, particularly for women. Women can be so indoctrinated with the idea that we need to 'do it all,' which is a throwback from generations past, mixed in with our own self-applied pressure.

More on that later.

There'll be different pieces in our lives that we need to work on at any given point in time.

It's like an onion, I always say; we keep peeling it away, and there's more to discover. Let's just hope we don't cry in the process!

But if we do, it's OK. we can always Receive support (see what I did there?).

So, as we begin to look at Receiving in your life right now, you could begin to find some hidden treasures.

The thing about Receiving, is it's a little bit like demisting the windows on your car windscreen.

The more that you see, the clearer it becomes to ask for what you want.

When everything feels misty and unclear, perhaps a bit foggy, we can ask for things and when they arrive, we might realise that it's not what we wanted at all – and that's okay.

We can return to the sender, we can pop them back in the returns bag, stick a label on it and say, "Thank you, that doesn't fit."

This is all about a journey.

This is all about demisting, clearing, and figuring out what works for you. After all, we are undoing layers and layers and layers and years of conditioning and habits and behaviours here.

So it's a little bit like sitting in your car with a cup of tea, letting things demist. It doesn't happen instantly.

It's a gradual process, so be kind to yourself.

The Mythology of 'Women's Work'
Even now, as I write this, women are still bearing the brunt of the responsibilities, chores, and emotional labour within the home.

I know, it's maddening, isn't it?

From the invisible, 'women's work' of childcare, grocery shopping, making doctors and dentists appointments (often for multiple people and generations) to taking care of gifts, family occasions, oh, and keeping a tidy house, well...we are knackered.

Not surprisingly.

The problem is quite complex.

Part of the issue is that patriarchy still has its claws in the ways that so many people think, and the perception of women as primary caregivers, homemakers, and nurturers has remained – despite the fact that we are now also out in the workforce as well – a shift in the working world that our grandparents simply wouldn't recognise.

But with this evolution in the way we live and work, the way we divide labour also needs to change in order for women, in particular, to not be still doing the work in our day jobs and the 'second shift' in the home.

We can begin by changing it in our own lives, and letting it ripple out.

Maybe, like Zara, you are so worn out from being the only one who takes care of the cooking, the washing, the cleaning, that not only is resentment building up towards your partner and your kids, but the idea that anyone will ever help feels just too out of reach.

It feels absolutely unthinkable that there might even be support available, let alone the capacity to receive it.

The dynamics of a household changes over time, too.

When my daughter and her boyfriend, now husband, came back to live with me for a while, I set the crystal clear boundary that I would no longer be doing her washing and ironing.

With three adults sharing a space, there was no way I was going to take on the work of washing for them both, and let them get used to having everything sorted for them. It took a little while before she realised I meant it (I did!), but she got the message and I didn't need to keep asking for help, or feeling resentment that I was doing it all.

Sometimes learning to Receive is as much about setting boundaries and clear ground rules for how you want to live, work and thrive, so that everyone is on the same page.

As you will find when we meander through this chapter, I might be sharing some harsh truths. But by now, you know how I roll, and you know it's said with love!

You might also find that as we uncover more areas that need work on Receiving, that you need to go back and repeat some steps of Clean, Let Go, Energise and Action.

You see, this work isn't linear. We can't tick it off and go about life with a certificate of completion (although I often wish Spirit would give me a badge or a certificate for each new level I reach!). No, this stuff is a reflective loop, and a process for self-discovery as you find more areas to go deeper.

Learning to Ask

Learning to Ask is one of the most important lessons when it comes to Receiving, for so many reasons.

Women, in particular, have been trained from the moment they are born to not Ask. If you think of all the things that are connotations of Asking, we are entrained and ingrained to feel that it's rude, or entitled, that we shouldn't be Asking for things. We are made to feel like it makes us seem conceited or demanding.

Really, all we are doing is articulating what we need, and Asking for it with clarity and an open heart.

That's it.

Doesn't that feel so different?

When we look at Receiving as it's related to Asking, it becomes really clear (pun intended!); if we find it difficult to Ask, it sends out the signal to other people and to the Universe that we also find it difficult to Receive.

We are energetically pushing that Receiving away by putting up barriers to Asking.

Things really change when you speak aloud your desires.

When you allow yourself to Ask for support, for love, for recognition, for what you need to thrive, it becomes far easier to Receive.

Of course this may take some practice, and you may need to Clear and Let Go of old beliefs, habits and experiences that have shown you that Asking does not get results.

A great place to start is to begin asking the Universe. I do this all the time – we need to give those guides and angels a job, after all!

If you find it hard to Ask the humans around you for what you need, start Asking the Universe, and begin noticing how that support comes in – because it will.

I am often found ranting and raging at Spirit (I love a bit of emotional charge to my requests), and then I hand it over. Without fail, when I ask and allow, I Receive.

Try it – what do you need to Ask for today?

Jeanne, who we've met often in this book, would say to me that she was Asking her guides for help. The way she said it just came across as so polite, it was so timid, like, "Oh, excuse me, angels, would you mind helping me?"

I got bolshy and Northern on her behalf, and told her to drop the nicey nicey tip toe approach.

After all, the Universe is there to support you.

Jeanne was dealing with a really difficult situation with her family, and was absolutely at her wit's end, and not feeling like any support was coming in from anywhere.

She started the CLEAR Method with a goal to begin shifting energy around this situation, as she began to clear her spaces and to Let Go of habits, beliefs, clutter and behaviours.

She started to Receive, and this really began with Letting Go of control, Letting Go of the need for certain outcomes.

In this particular case, she really wanted her siblings to step up and support her. But we have no control over how other people behave and how other people react. They are on their own journey after all.

So I advised her to hand it over to the Universe, to just literally use all that fury, all that rage, and demand support from the Universe. I told her, "Just say that you cannot do this on your own," and hand it over.

Maybe this resonates with you?

Maybe you have had moments where you just feel like there's no-one there to help you, no-one to support you, and you just don't know where help is going to come from.

Well, this is when we can use Receiving from the Universe. It's the most powerful thing we can Ask for, and guess what? We don't need to know how support will come in.

The Universe is full of ways to surprise and to guide us and to offer us support.

All we need to do is Ask, and yes, rant and rave at the Universe.

Tell them how you feel.

Speak it aloud.

Ask for that support, while you Let Go of how that outcome arrives.

Remember, this is all a dance in the CLEAR Method, isn't it?

We are Asking whilst Letting Go, we are Receiving whilst Clearing.

Jeanne really took it to heart. She expressed with rage and fury how she felt alone in caring for her Mum. She expressed that she needed help, that she was willing to Let Go of the outcome, and she said it aloud to the Universe, her guides, and Spirit.

In fact, she really had a good rant about it in her home, as she told me. This not only Energised the situation by Letting Go and fuelling it with emotion, but it also acted as a kind of ceremony, in a way, to invite in more support. Which is exactly what happened, by the way.

You see, the Universe does show up when we Ask it to, and if we allow it to.

Suddenly appointments that she'd been trying to book for months and months began to appear in her diary for support.

She bumped into someone in the local café who ran a business that could help support her.

She began finding out about ways where that support could arrive.

And, when the people did show up to support her, they were absolutely lovely!

Now, did her siblings show up to help? Not at first, no. They weren't the ones that showed up. But when she Let Go of the outcome, allowed other ways to come in, and spoke it aloud, other support did come.

Speaking things aloud has such an energy to it.

Especially when we use emotions behind things. Life is full of roller coaster moments, isn't it? We have grief, sadness, loss, anger, hurt. And actually, all those emotions, those times of energy in emotion, which is all that an emotion is, are there to help us.

We can use that energy to move through and to ask for what we need.

Receiving and Letting Go are so interlinked. But all the elements of the CLEAR Method are, if we're honest about it, everything is so intertwined, because it is all a dance.

As I've said before, none of this is linear, as you will discover, as your CLEARing gets underway.

Some things for you to consider:

- How easy do you find it to Ask for help?

- How easy do you find it to speak aloud what you need?

- Can you practise Asking friends, family, and people close to you, colleagues, for what you need without apology?

- Can you utilise all that energy, or that anger, fear, grief and frustration that will appear in your life to harness some change, to motivate you to demand that something changes?

- And can you Let Go of the outcome?

- Ask aloud for what you need without apology, and with full intention that you will Receive it.

- Can you feel that shift in you? Amazing.

Now, watch how it all comes in (and don't forget to tag me on social media @carolynspiritual when it does).

Denying People the Joy of Giving

The thing about learning to Receive is that by doing so, we are gifting others.

You see, there is joy when we gift and offer our support – resources, love, presence – from a place of real meaning and intention.

When you struggle to Receive, you're actually denying other people that joy.

Try thinking about it that way; maybe it helps whenever you are struggling to Receive.

Remember that it lifts us all up.

Think about the random acts of kindness idea, if you've ever taken part in that. Yes, of course the recipient of the kindness benefits, but so do you, the giver.

Every time you've offered help from a real depth in your heart, or you've given a birthday gift to someone that you really love, think about that feeling. That's what you are blocking in the person who was trying to help you if you push the gift back.

We've all been in a restaurant where someone has tried to pay the bill and the fight that ensues is often not only undignified, but also embarrassing and immediately removes the altruism of the person trying to pay.

Of course this is a journey, learning when to Receive.

One of my clients, Nadine, is a great Mum and business woman – control freak she would say, actually! Spinning all the plates. You know the type of woman – a human whirlwind – intent on nailing herself to the cross. Until one day her back went – proper spasms and unable to move, type of back pain. She admitted to me that she had experienced twinges but hadn't paid attention to what her body and spirit had been sharing.

Spirit had been nudging her for a little to slow down, ask for and Receive help. But she (like many of us) thought she knew best. She could handle it. So Spirit (or her grandmother, I later realised) jabbed her in the back, so she had no choice but to stop and Receive help.

It meant she needed to explain to the children how they could help her by helping themselves. The children she had been mollycoddling, soon figured out how to get dressed themselves, take their plates into the kitchen and clear up after themselves. Grandparents were over the moon to have their grandchildren stay while Mum rested her back for a few days.

Funnily enough once Nadine stopped, rested and began to Receive the help with grace (instead of rejecting it and fighting it grumpily on the sofa), the back pain eased off. She also realised just because she could be all things, didn't mean she had to. She has a much more healthy relationship with her kids as a result. And instead of feeling like it's a burden for the Grandparents to look after the children, she now knows that helping her; helps them. Because they get to have fun with their Grandchildren – a joy they love to Receive.

Again, let's think about those boundaries being in place, and learning how to Receive might take some time. After all, we've been conditioned to push things away to do on our own, and to feel weak if we accept help, or that gifts are somehow bribes that are laden with meaning.

So many of these things are infused in our culture in a way that is far from positive, and it takes time to undo that.

The clearer you get, the more connected to your higher self you get, the easier that becomes, and we open ourselves up to Receiving from the right people, in the right way, at the right time.

What if it feels like nothing is coming?

What if it feels like you just can't see the help that you are asking for?

This is where we need to get back to Energising and Activating. Harness those emotions, really step into your rage, your fury, your anger.

The Universe responds to those emotions. In fact, they're like a portal. So next time you feel let down, alone, as if no-one is listening, take it to the Universe.

As I always say, they're in charge of my life now, not me. I put the angels, my guides, the Universe in charge. That relinquishes me of all responsibility.

Every time I'm feeling as if there's no help, as if I'm stuck, as if everything is on me, I pass it back on to them (often with a good old Yorkshire rant).

So, Energise your requests with emotions.

Ask – in fact, demand – and see how you're receiving shifts when you activate it and infuse it with that energy.

The Responsibility of Receiving

Working with Receiving is a real journey in itself, as I am sure you have already discovered by now, in some way or another, just by the fact of being human!

When it comes to Receiving, we can't be fully open to Receiving and, equally importantly, being able to hold onto what we Receive, if we haven't done the groundwork.

What do I mean by that?

Well, have you ever seen those shows where a team goes in to clear out the homes of people who hoard items? Often, they clear all the stuff, it looks like new, but in a few weeks or months it's right back to the state it started in. (Maybe you have met some people like that in your own life? I know I have).

So why does it always return back to the state it was previously in?

Well, the occupants of the house hadn't taken on the responsibility themselves; they hadn't gone through the motions of energetically Clearing their spaces, and Letting Go of the belongings on an energetic level, in order to be open to fully Receiving the support and changing their habits for good.

We can't fix people for them, however tempting it is to want to try! And believe me, I know it can be tempting.

Responsibility is SO important. We all need to take responsibility for our own actions, and that might sound really obvious, but this becomes particularly clear – if you pardon the pun – when it comes to Receiving.

Because this is the part where we see the results of our actions – of our Clearing, Letting Go, Energising.

When it comes to Receiving, whether it's wisdom, money, freedom, time, love or support, if we haven't taken responsibility for the steps that got us to be able to Receive, it's unlikely we'll be able to hold on to what we Receive for very long.

Also, we gain resilience through the process of Clearing. After all, by going through those energetic shifts of Clearing and Letting Go, Energising and Activating, some really profound changes take place in our energetic field.

In short, we are doing the work. It turns out, sorry to say this, but you just can't shortcut that. I know, not even with a life hack. Not even with a cleaning hack.

This stuff does require us to be present and to partake in it.

We can't outsource this stuff.

Now a word on that. Yes, *of course* you can outsource your cleaning. You can absolutely get someone to come and help keep your home nice and clean, make sure that your surfaces are dust free, that your carpets have lovely lines on them, and that your home is running in a way that feels good without you having to do everything.

I built a big business, and I wouldn't have been able to do that without Letting Go and delegating the day to day cleaning of my house. You don't become the boss of a cleaning company by continuing to clean the toilets...

But – and here is the crux of it – you can't delegate the Clearing.

The CLEAR Method piece of this is personal... It's where Receiving can really happen, and it's where resilience is born. It's where we re-energise and reconnect with ourselves – the proof is in the pudding, if you like.

So, yes, we can get support to keep our spaces clean but the actual energetic CLEARing just can't be fast tracked.

In the same way that we want our kids to learn, we have to let them go through the process of discovery themselves.

There is always more to uncover when it comes to Receiving.

If someone sweeps in and tries to fix it for you, you can't be empowered, embodied and energised to Receive the end result.

Receiving is the ultimate test, if you like, of doing the process.

Have you really Let Go?

Have you cleared out what's holding you back ?

Have you decluttered your spaces, your energy, and anything that has been attached to your field that you no longer need?

Now of course, as I mentioned at the start of this book, this is a dance, you'll likely be hopping between Clearing, Energising, Letting Go, Activating and Receiving at any one point in time with various different pieces of the work in progress.

But remember, it's at the Receiving end of things that we can really have a measure of how we are doing. It's like a barometer of the CLEAR Method, in a way.

If you have called something in, if you're trying to manifest something new in your life, or trying to reach a goal and it's just not happening, then you probably need to go back and revisit, and look into why that is.

Maybe the goal isn't yours.

Maybe it doesn't truly resonate with you.

Maybe you haven't Let Go of something else.

Where we can really put the microscope on things is in the Receiving piece.

It's hard, I know.

But it's also really wonderful when you do begin to see and Receive all the things that you're calling into your life, plus much, much more than you can ever have imagined.

So trust me on this. This work does take responsibility, but it's so, so worth it.

Before we start this chapter, as always, we're going to check in with a little CLEAR Method meditation, specifically to check in with where you might need to focus first on Receiving.

Meditation

So find yourself sitting somewhere really comfortable.

Focus on your body being supported, with the seat beneath you, or the Earth beneath your feet.

Visualise your feet planted firmly on the ground, with roots growing from them all the way down into the centre of the Earth, growing your roots, earthing you right into the core of the Earth.

Feel those tendrils of your strong tree roots underneath your feet, planted, spiralling way down into the centre.

Now imagine a white light connected from the top of your head that goes far, far, far right up into the heavens, as far as you can imagine, into infinity, this beautiful, bright white light.

Now, you are connected to all that is. And as you breathe in, you can feel the white light pulling down from the heavens into your crown.

As you breathe out, you are flushing anything that you do not need into the earth, where Mother Earth transmutes anything that no longer serves you.

Now, imagine yourself shrinking down to a teeny, tiny version of yourself, and choose the cleaning method that you would like to use today.

Maybe you're sweeping, maybe you're polishing, maybe you're hoovering, maybe you are washing, spraying. Whichever one you choose, pick a method that feels right for you today, and start in your Crown Chakra, the area right at the top of your head.

Imagine the tiny version of you is up there, spraying away or cleaning away anything that's no longer needed all around your Crown.

When you feel your Crown area is clear, move down to your Third Eye.

Give it a wipe, or a polish, a sweep - however that tiny version of you is cleaning away anything in the area between your eyebrows that no longer serves you, that no longer is needed.

Moving on down to your Throat, clearing away, polishing it up, hoovering away the debris right at the front of your throat. Little You is clearing away anything that you no longer need.

Now move on down to your Heart space. See yourself dusting away, spraying, hoovering right in front of your Heart before you move down to your Solar Plexus - clearing everything, making space until you find ourselves at your Sacral Chakra, right down in your belly. Into your pelvis clearing, clearing, clearing, and then down to your Root right at the bottom of your perineum.

Little You is vacuuming, clearing, dusting away, and we know that Mother Earth is taking all the debris that we've cleaned out right down through those tree roots, sucking right out of your energetic field anything that you no longer need.

When you feel that your Mini You has cleaned everywhere, take a few deep, cleansing breaths in through the nose.

Let it all out through the mouth, before returning to scan your body as a whole and just feel with your intuition, with your inner knowing.

When you think of the word 'receiving,' and how it feels to Receive, where do you feel some resistance in your body?

Which part of your body feels tight, constricted, or compressed?

Spend a moment recognising that feeling, and trust that the answer that you get is right for you right now.

It might change every time, trusting that your body knows, your higher self knows.

Take another deep breath, and begin to move your body to reconnect with the space that you are in.

Readiness to Receive Quiz

OK, as always, let's check in with your readiness and capacity to Receive, before we explore this part of the CLEAR Method together.

Let's acknowledge again here, because it's always worth repeating, that this work will always uncover more for you as you go deeper.

Do this quiz now, and feel into how it compares with how your body felt after the meditation. Work on where you need to allow more receiving in right now, and come back often to unlock more, when the time is right. You will know when that is (trust me, I'm a psychic!).

Questions

1 - You are meeting a friend for a catch up, and they are ordering coffee. Your friend asks what you would like to drink, and that it's on them as a gift. Do you:

    A - Say, "Thank you! How kind. A cappuccino for me, please!"

    B - Panic, grab your wallet from your bag, wave your cash or card to the barista and say, "No, let ME get this!"

    C - Say, "Are you sure?" five or six times, then make it known that the next time is on you and remain deeply uncomfortable for the whole time you are catching up. The guilt is just so distracting!

2 - You are having a really busy week. Work is busy, your

family has a lot of commitments in the diary, and there is still the washing, cooking, and shopping to be done. Do you:

    A - Make a big list, decide what you can do and what you can't, ask for help, and happily receive it.

    B - Get on with it all yourself, seething with resentment, and feeling utterly shattered.

    C - Murmur to your family about how much you are doing, and when people offer help, vaguely accept it but still do the bulk of the load yourself.

3 - You arrive at a party, and your friend compliments you on your outfit. Do you:

    A - Say, "Thank you! I love this colour!"

    B - Launch into a 2 minute monologue about how you look really fat/old/tired, that you need to lose weight, or that you got the dress in the sale.

    C - Vaguely acknowledge the compliment, then deflect it to compliment your friend in return.

4 - You find out that an elderly relative has left you some money in their will after they have passed away. Do you:

    A - Celebrate this incredible gift. Invest some, gift some to a cause that you love, and spend the rest on doing something you have always wanted to do.

    B - Plan how to spend it on everyone else, the guilt of having it is just too much. You don't deserve it after all.

    C - Worry about it until it has gradually gone, but you feel too bad to really enjoy it.

5 - Your partner offers to cook you a meal and to run a bath for you so you can relax before enjoying some time together. Do you:

A - Relish the offer of support and closeness, and let them know your favourite meal and bath bomb?

B - Insist that you cook for them, after all their job is far more important than yours.

C - Enjoy the bath and meal, but spend the whole time feeling guilty and saying how wonderful your partner is.

6 - Your colleague makes a point of letting your team know how well you did on a project during a meeting. Do you:

A - Enjoy the recognition, share what you learned, and glow in the gratitude of being seen and acknowledged.

B - Deflect the praise back to your colleague (you hate all this attention, and after all, did you really do that much?)

C - Blush profusely, end the meeting as soon as possible, and murmur your embarrassed thanks.

Mainly As:

You are pretty good at Receiving. Well done! There is always more to uncover, to stay aware of areas in your life where you could be more open to allowing in even more abundance of praise, support, and wealth. Take a look at the section called 'Gifts on Tap from the Universe' for ways to experiment with Receiving more.

Mainly Bs:

OK, you are in need of Receiving 101. You need to start with some baby steps to get used to receiving, asking, and joyfully holding what is sent your way.

Mainly Cs:

You are open to Receiving but find it difficult and uncomfortable. Often this is around an old story, a childhood belief that has stayed with you, or other people's limitations. Take a look forward at the 'Tap, Receive, Repeat,' section and start to open up more to all the abundance that awaits you.

Receiving 101: The Five Day Receiving Challenge

Sometimes, as with anything, we just need to go back to basics.

Receiving 101 is a way to get started back with the idea of Receiving; I say get started, because when you were a child you knew how to Receive.

Did you ever turn down love as a child, or a gift ,or words of praise?

It's only as we grow up and we inherit and take on beliefs, habits and behaviours that we push away things that come towards us.

So, 'Receiving 101' is our little experiment to get you back into the mode of Receiving.

Part of this is about enabling your nervous system to hold what's coming your way, and to make it safe for you to Receive.

We do that by gently regulating your nervous system as you Receive more, and to begin getting playful with situations where you can put Receiving to the test.

So, here's a five day experiment to begin inviting Receiving back into your life. It's a way to begin re-setting the habit, and to turn the big old universal tap on to Receive.

Now, you may wish to extend this to 30 days or 60 days or a longer time to really help embed the habit of receiving - because that's what it really is, a habit.

Once it becomes a habit, it becomes a behaviour. It becomes part of you.

But to get started, we're going to look at baby steps just to get you back into being mindful of your reactions towards receiving, and taking steps to allow more in .

Day 1:

As you start the day, in your journal note down your intentions for the day.

Where do you need support? Where would you love to feel loved?

Where could you use encouragement, or more of anything – be it more income, more time, freedom, whatever it is that you need.

Notice what it is that you feel you would love to Receive, and note it down.

Set that clear intention, and put it out to the Universe – after all, they're in charge! *I love handing things over to the Universe, that's what it's here for. We are surrounded by guides and angels and Spirit who want to help us, so let's give them a job shall we?*

Throughout the day, notice and be open to opportunities to Receive.

Maybe it's something like someone offering you a coffee, or offering you words of praise. Maybe you are gifted a book, a place on a course, or given the chance to jump ahead in a queue.

Whatever it is, it'll be different for each of us as we go through this experiment.

Be mindful, be open, and practice feeling in your body how it feels to accept (whilst also remaining within your personal boundaries and what feels good to say yes to, of course).

At the end of the day, review where you have had an opportunity to Receive today.

Notice how it felt.

Were you able to Receive without guilt, shame, and a sense of burden?

What did you notice about Receiving today?

Where did you feel Receiving in your body?

Now do something to soothe your nervous system.

You might want to choose a yoga nidra meditation (there are plenty on YouTube that are excellent).

You might want to spend some time relaxing in the bath, or you might want to do some breathwork.

The more that we open up our capacity to Receive, the more we need to regulate our nervous system, in order to be able to hold what is coming towards us.

So, make sure you spend some time today celebrating whatever you have Received, and also regulating your nervous system so that you can continue to hold, and that you feel safe to keep on Receiving.

We're retraining your mind, your habits, and your nervous system to Receive here, and it's an ongoing practice.

It's a marathon, not a sprint.

Day 2:
What are your intentions for today?

What would you *love* to Receive?

Would you love to Receive time? Would you love to Receive words of encouragement? Or maybe you just want to keep it open and let the Universe choose?

Set that intention in your journal. Feel it in your body, and go about your day - we need to get used to handing things over to the Universe.

Maybe you find today that you're slightly more aware of opportunities to Receive.

Maybe there's a little feeling of excitement.

Notice it as you go about your day.

In the evening when you do your review, sit down. Nurture yourself in some way; perhaps you have a mug of cocoa, or light a candle while you review your day, feeling where you have been able to Receive, and what has felt like a successful Receiving experiment today.

Where have you said yes? What has surprised you?

Where did you feel it in your body?

Now, choose another nurturing exercise to really show your nervous system that Receiving is safe.

You might choose from simply reading a book and tucking yourself up with your favourite warm drink, or to switch off your phone and spend some time in your hammock, or walking in nature.

Whatever it is, soothe yourself.

Remind your body that it's safe to Receive; we are relearning again, after all.

———————————————

Day 3:
How do you feel this morning as you approach your journal?

Do you feel excited about the idea of Receiving as we begin to reset this habit? Sometimes it just feels really weird to bring in that element of fun – remember Receiving is a gorgeous thing.

We are divine creatures with the right to infinite abundance, and once we begin to reopen that abundance, remembering all that is available to us can really open up some more excitement.

Today, I want you to start dreaming.

Often when we get stuck in our mindsets and habits, we forget to dream. If dreaming BIG, really big, feels difficult, maybe just dream a little bit bigger.

What would you love your life to look like a month from now, three months from now, a year from now?

Where would you love to feel supported and abundant?

Again, this doesn't need to be monetary, this can be an abundance of creativity, an abundance of time, an abundance of love, an abundance of wealth, of energy, whatever it is that you tune into right now.

Journal it down, and again set the intention that you are open to Receive from the Universe today.

Be open to how that might show up throughout the day. Be mindful of those opportunities to Receive, and how it feels to say yes, to be open, playful, excited.

Can you feel that shift in your energy when you review your day?

Can you feel a sense of your energy shifting towards Receiving?

Have you noticed the way that the Universe is now starting to honour this assignment of being aware?

Again, do what you can to nourish your nervous system, even if it is just three deep, conscious breaths.

This is something you can bring with you throughout the day, whenever your nervous system feels a bit jingly, or whenever you've taken a big step towards doing something new, taking three deep, conscious breaths is something you can do wherever you are.

Day 4:
Let's really get the Universe to surprise you today.

Invite the Universe to send you the most unexpected gift, and be open to however that might show up for you.

Sometimes we need to play with not being attached to any outcome at all, but simply being open to Receiving, to flex that muscle.

Set the intention as you start your day in your journal, in your heart, in your mind. and go about your day.

In your evening review, what showed up for you? How were you gifted, what did you Receive? How do you feel about it? How do you feel about playing this game?

How is the week feeling for you?

Again, choose another activity to nurture yourself.

Day 5:
We're on the homestretch now.

In this little experiment, we've just taken some time to really feel into Receiving, to play with the possibility of opening your arms, your heart, your mind and soul to the possibility of more.

Sometimes it looks like something we're deliberately calling in.

Sometimes we're calling in just the energy of Receiving, because when we practise Receiving in all areas, it opens us up in other areas of life too.

How have you felt about Receiving this week as we look back?

How's your body been feeling?

What have you noticed about how you've changed, even if it's just a tiny shift towards being more mindful that Receiving is an option for you?

Note down what comes up for you when you feel into this week and how it's gone.

I would love to hear how you have moved through this experiment, so please come and share and tag me over on social media on @carolynspiritual on Instagram, or you can send me an email or a message. I would love to Receive (see what I did there?!) your news, and your results of your own experiment.

Today for the final day, see if you can dial things up just a little bit more.

Set your intention with the Universe that you are ready to Receive something that you've been scared of Receiving before, whatever that might be for you.

Maybe it's a big pay rise, maybe it's support from somebody that you love who never shows up for you. Maybe it's lunch at Harrods, a bar of chocolate. Whatever it is, set the intention that you are open to Receiving, that you are here with open arms, open heart, open mind, and see what the Universe brings you.

At the end of the day, celebrate this week.

Celebrate that you've taken time to begin undoing some habits that were learned in childhood, where you began to believe that Receiving wasn't possible for you.

Has this experiment begun to turn that around for you?

I really hope so.

It's something that I come back to often myself, and something that's really simple and playful and creative.

See, Receiving can be fun! Honestly.

Tap, Receive, Repeat

Sometimes, even though we have the basics of Receiving down, we need to really revisit our capacity to Receive and our capacity to hold onto whatever we are gifted.

Now, although we've done a lot of work on Letting Go and Clearing, there are some things that we do want to hold on to - love, wealth, abundance, when they come our way.

So pay attention to things that come into your life that you do Receive, and really we are looking at supporting your body, your mind, your nervous system in being open to more, by just turning up that Receiving dial a little bit more. And being able to hold it so that you don't immediately get rid of all the money from your pay rise, or all the gifts that come your way.

A great tool for helping you is EFT.

I love EFT – as much as I think that counselling and therapy are really good, and useful for many people, EFT for me just gets straight to the root of the problem really quickly.

If you have never encountered EFT before, it's called Emotional Freedom Technique. It's a methodology that helps to clear limiting beliefs, and stagnant energy by tapping on the meridians of the body.

You don't even necessarily know what you're clearing, because you're working on the spiritual, energetic, and emotional level.

What I want for you to do, having got your Receiving 101 in place, is to build a daily habit over the next few days of spending five or 10 minutes tapping, to open up to your ability to receive a little bit more, and to feel safe as you do so.

As with all these things, it's about setting the habit. So, as you begin resetting your ability to Receive, you can support yourself by putting on your calendar, 5 to 10 minutes every day for the next 5 days to give yourself the time to tap.

Begin by tapping on the karate chop point, which is a side of your left hand, just with the tips of the fingers of your right hand.

Repeat as you tap, "It's safe to Receive. It's safe to Receive. It's safe to Receive."

Now, tap on the top of your head right where your Crown Chakra is, and use the phrase, "Even though I'm re-learning to Receive, it's safe to Receive even more."

Tap on that point for 30 seconds or so.

Move to the side of the eye, just above your eyebrow. As you tap there, repeat the phrase, "I'm open to Receiving, and I'm open to holding more without guilt, without shame, without fear."

Move on down to your top lip, just below the nose.

As you tap there, repeat the phrase

"I can Receive without judgement, without fear, without shame, even though in the past I've struggled with Receiving. I am clearing it all now. I'm clearing it throughout my body, my nervous system, my heart and my soul."

Move to your chest, just by your clavicle area.

Tap on that point, repeating the phrase, "Receiving feels safe in my body. I Let Go of all the things that have held me back from Receiving. I am safe, I am here. I am loved."

Now repeat that cycle for a few times.

This is a tool you can use and come back to whenever you are working on Receiving more in your life.

The more we Receive, the more we adjust to that capacity of Receiving and we can keep moving that threshold towards the infinite abundance that is available to us.

It takes a little bit of work, because this is all a work in progress.

But by using EFT, you can move through it quickly and efficiently, and you can get to the point where you're Receiving so much more in your life.

You'll be amazed at how you got here.

Gifts on Tap from the Universe

Once you are fairly used to Receiving and your nervous system is getting accustomed to holding gifts and inviting them more, you can really dial up how much you play.

This is where you can start to get super creative, and see how far you can dream, how much you can invite in and be open to.

This is an invitation to get super playful.

You might want to set an intention in the morning to Receive the most surprising, extravagant, unexpected gift, and see what the Universe delivers for you each time, because it will.

You've done the groundwork. You're working on assimilating and Receiving in your body. You're working on being open to holding more and more. Now you can get really creative.

Ask the Universe every day for an unexpected gift, and celebrate it every time it comes.

The more you send out the message that you are open to Receiving and that you are open to inviting in more, the more fun you can have with this.

Often, I find that people just forget to do this. To be fair, I thought we all had that contact and relationship with Spirit. They are always there. Many of us forget that we have the ability to call in cool stuff from Spirit.

That's what they're there for!

They're there not only to help you with the daily grind in the day to day – one of my clients loves to call the 'parking angels' – but also to really make your life magical.

You have infinite powers to call in anything anytime.

Sometimes I really love to let them surprise me.

My client Jo played this game once and invited the Universe to send her an unexpected gift in the post.

Just a day or so later, a friend sent her a helium unicorn balloon through the post. How funny is that?

You see the Universe does have a sense of humour. Keep a log of what shows up for you.

The more you keep evidence of what happens, it's like proving to your logical mind and your consciousness that this stuff really really works.

It does.

We just need to keep seeing it and believing it and repeating it.

So get creative with your experiments and make sure that you can tag me on social media @carolynspiritual, or send me an email and share with me your stories of the exciting things that the Universe is sending you.

I can't wait to hear. I can't wait to Receive what works for you and to share your stories.

Receiving Guidance – decluttered thinking

Receiving with Infinity (and Boundaries)

It feels right to pause here and just note that as we work on Receiving, we begin to see how all the sections of the CLEAR Method are so interlinked.

Receiving without boundaries and discernment opens us up to even more clutter; whether that's a clutter of opinions, of visitors, of items arriving in your house, of thoughts. Whatever it is, when we Receive, we also need to apply a filter.

Imagine it a little bit like the filter in your tumble dryer that catches all the fluff. We need to be like that in our own lives, and clear it out on a regular basis.

Because just like that fluff on the filter in your tumble dryer, we can become clogged when we Receive things that we are not necessarily consciously inviting in.

For example, Jo's family grew up with a single mother on income support.

Her grandparents were incredibly generous and supported by bringing in all sorts of things to help the family with their weekly shop.

They would turn up every week with bags of shopping and supplies for the family.

However, they would also bring in last week's newspapers, and anything that her Nan had found on one of her infamous jumble sale hauls.

Now, Jo was also a fan of jumble sales, but the sheer amount of stuff coming into her room and into her house was already becoming untenable.

Her Mum, struggling with the stress of divorce and bringing up three kids on her own, was developing a real tendency for hoarding, springing from the 'make do and mend' mentality that lots of baby boomer wartime babies often fall into. Coupled with living in poverty and being worried there would never be 'enough,' she would hold onto things.

This meant that all of the newspapers that were brought into the house rarely went back out again, and gathered dust in heaps scattered throughout the living room.

All of the clothes that her grandparents bought 'just in case' for the kids, often didn't go back out again.

Jo began to realise this, and tried to put a boundary in place in her teenage years.

The next time her Nan brought in an item of clothing that she really didn't want, she thanked her Nan kindly and said, "Thank you very much, but that's not for me."

Her Nan was deeply offended, and it became more problematic to set the boundary than not, so Jo learned at a very young age that we Receive without boundaries.

And of course, this has a knock-on effect through so many areas of life.

Learning to put boundaries in place means that we need to do less decluttering, because we've already popped that filter in.

Those filters need revisiting over and over again, as we grow, as we evolve, and as we change as humans.

The CLEAR Method is never linear.

It's an ongoing process of weaving between Clearing, Letting Go, Energising, Activating and Receiving – sometimes within one area at a time, sometimes all at once.

It's about understanding how to ebb and flow between all of them.

The more that you step into this method, and the more that you are aware of the different steps, the different areas, the easier it becomes.

Things to journal and reflect on:
Where have you found it difficult to initiate a boundary?

Where have you tried to set a boundary in the past, and it has been ignored?

As a child, were you able to say what you needed, and to pop a boundary in place around your belongings, your body, your time?

How does it feel now as an adult?

For further reading on boundaries, there's an excellent book called *Set Boundaries, Find Peace* by Nedra Glover Tawaab.

Psychic Connection

Another really important note around Receiving and boundaries matters when it comes to your psychic connection.

As you journey through the CLEAR Method dance space and your psychic connection deepens, it's important to lay down some boundaries with whatever or whoever is coming through.

Sometimes, a deepened sense of connection can lead to a flurry of ideas waking you up at night.

Anyone who is creative will know this process only too well.

Or, the speed at which opportunities, projects, people and new beginnings start to come in can feel like a tap on full blast.

Maybe you begin to have a sense of Spirit all around you, or your dreams are becoming vivid, and are filled with messages and meetings with other people, realms and beings.

All these things are signs that your psychic connection – that awareness and connection to the Universe – is opening up, your Third Eye is clearing, you are plugged in, and knowledge is flowing.

But, what if it's flying too fast?

Sometimes it can feel like we are on a supernatural highway of creativity and opportunity. This can feel absolutely incredible, but we are only human after all.

Firstly, you can ask Spirit at any time to slow things down for you. Ask them to make this connection more manageable.

If the ideas, invitations and things you are Receiving are just too much, set a boundary. Yes, even the Spirit World needs some boundaries to be set! I do it all the time. You can absolutely ask Spirit to slow their roll. Honestly, they do respond to this and the Universe is here to support you.

So you can absolutely ask for things to be given to you in a way that's easier to Receive.

Perhaps you need things slower; perhaps you need things in a different way – just ask them and they will support you.

In meditation, imagine grounding yourself to help bring you down to earth, is your connection to the upper realms feels too floaty and fast.

You can also close down your Third Eye just a little bit. It's just between your eyebrows. Imagine just making the circle there a little smaller to close down the connection.

It's OK to slow down and to give yourself a breather from the connection.

We actually do get to Receive in a way that works for us.

Whilst going through the CLEAR Method, Leanne was writing a book.

Like most creative entities, this book had an energy of its own. It began to arrive in her awareness first thing in the morning when she woke up, with words, concepts, and whole pages coming through asking to be written.

She began to set boundaries with it, asking it to please come back later when she had had her coffee, and she would happily sit down with it and let it all come through.

When I do readings for clients, I have to set clear boundaries with Spirit, as I would constantly be attached to the Spirit Realm and be burned out by Receiving messages all day and night from people on the other side wanting to get through.

I have to set a clear boundary with them that they are to leave me alone after our connection together.

Creating clear psychic boundaries for the Spirit World is one thing, and it's part of being a medium.

Setting energetic boundaries, as well as physical ones, are important parts of the CLEAR Method journey.

If it all feels too much, slow it down. Chat to Spirit. They are there to help you.

Summary

Now you have learned the art of Receiving in all its facets.

I wonder how that has changed your life? Are you calling in the parking angels, or finally accepting help like Nadine?

I'd really love to know – I'm nosey and I really would appreciate any stories you wish to share.

I know learning to Receive has changed my life.

I'll be honest, I still struggle to Receive at times, but knowing that is something I need to constantly work on is half the battle!

Thank you for sticking it out and getting to this point. And I know I have said this several times, but it is a constant dance, this CLEAR Method.

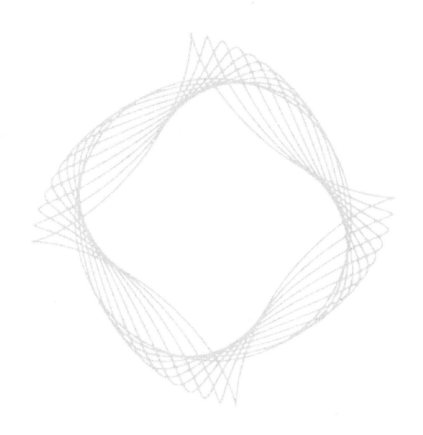

The Power of CLEARing to Create Your Own Hope in Uncertain Times

The times we live in right now are nothing short of continually surprising, aren't they?

Over the last few years, we've seen all sorts of things shaking us to the very core of our existence.

However we live our lives, and whoever we are, we've all been affected in one way or another.

Uncertainty is difficult.

Uncertainty is the perfect breeding ground for fear, mistrust, doubt, and a real sense of lacking.

And there's no doubt that for many, many people, their lives have been changed beyond all recognition.

With the world in an ever-increasing state of chaos, is there anything we can do?

I truly believe that the way we choose to react and create our own lives is the pathway to hope.

What we do have control over is:

- Navigating the way we feel

- How we set up our own emotions and nervous system

- Our intuition and the way we live our lives.

We always have choices: even in the tiniest of ways, and when it feels like we don't.

I've navigated many difficult things throughout my life.

No one reaches my age without some stories – and believe me, I have many, some of which I have shared with you within these pages.

My experience of growing a business, raising a family, and coming through some of the most difficult times, shows me that we can create our own hope by taking steps to love ourselves just a little bit more.

And that isn't an airy fairy, nebulous term – loving ourselves means giving ourselves hope, and finding strength in the things that light us up and make us feel excited inside.

What brings you joy?

Incorporating those things into your life, even in the smallest of ways, is so empowering.

Creating hope for yourself and trusting there's a future that's exciting and bright is so transformative.

First of all, you need to take the time to dream and consider how you'd like your life to look.

How would you like your days to feel?

How do you want to spend your time, and with whom?

We often forget to dream, and appreciate that we can put things in place to change our lives.

Clearing your space may feel like a futile act when the world is in chaos, and so many people are struggling.

But if we can change our own lives in the smallest of ways, it really does have a ripple effect that goes out into the world in the most profound way.

Think about your own inner circle: if you clear your space, connect to your intuition, and create the life you love (and in which you thrive), you affect the people around you.

Show them how to do the same; share that joy and hope.

When it feels like you can't take control of anything, you can control your own sense of wellbeing and hope.

The CLEAR Method is a great way to start.

Begin in the tiniest of ways by setting yourself goals to clear areas of your home, freeing up energy to Receive more joy and hope.

Clearing spaces of clutter also releases the old stories, the old energies, and the old pieces of you that no longer fit into the life you're building.

Hope can still exist in the most uncertain times.

Finding it requires you to make room to get clear in every way.

A Note on The Rise of the 'Cleanfluencers'

Cleaning supplies are flying off the shelves from being recommended on Instagram, and whether it's a #FreshupFriday or an every #Hinching moment, cleaning is taking social media by storm.

In fact, a recent academic study took a deep dive into the current rise of what they are calling 'Cleanfluencers' – the Mrs Hinch's and the like – and the cultural forces driving this trend to glamorise the daily clean.

Here's what the Cleanfluencers are missing – the spiritual effect that clearing their spaces has on their lives.

We are glamorising domestic work and it's big business. But there is a deeper reason behind the Cleanfluencer meteoric rise – and it's more to do with energy and spiritual connection than bleach and Zoflora.

Listen, I run a cleaning business. I should be all over this stuff.

Right?

Well, not quite.

Let's stop for a moment and just look at a few things, shall we?

Firstly, I am all for people enjoying their cleaning. I LOVE that there is such a movement around this, and I know that so many people are experiencing the benefits of parts of the CLEAR Method without necessarily knowing why.

What I am not keen on is:

1 - The promotion of ALL the products, all the time.

Listen, we don't need all the things to Clean and CLEAR. The very minimum works, and a microfibre towel with some water goes a long way, let me tell you.

2 - Forgetting sustainability.

This is an issue that in the Cleanfluencer corner of the world we seem to have forgotten. Let's be mindful of how much plastic we are using, and just how many chemicals we are putting in our homes. Reduce, reuse, recycle – remember that? We need to.

3 - The over consumption of cleaning products.

Buying more leads to overconsumption of 'stuff,' and cupboards full of cleaning products that may or may not be in use, but they are what the latest Instagram Cleanfluencer has convinced us to buy.

4 - The danger of cleaning anxiety and OCD.
Following other people's lives on social media is a minefield, full stop. If you are already experiencing overwhelm, anxiety, fatigue, and wheel-spinning in your daily life, adding the pressure of comparison is going to add extra pressure on you. For anyone with a tendency to mask mental health challenges with external behaviours, this can also be a slippery slope to more anxiety, and even OCD. Be mindful.

5 - Buying cupboards full of The Pink Stuff and Zoflora won't give you their lives and a big house.

Whatever you are seeing on social media isn't real life in full range. Remember that. It's often easier to avoid the issues going on in your own world by aspiring to someone else's life.

6 - We are glamorising domestic work, predominantly for females.

We have come a long way since the 1950s. I won't say too much on this, but just be aware that glamorising women doing housework is adding so much pressure back on that we had worked so hard to lose and to CLEAR.

Final Thoughts

"You may journey through waterfalls, rapids and floods,
stagnation, strong undercurrents and the sheer terror of
drowning at times.
But the magic is in the moments.
It's the glimmering diamonds of light that dance off the waves.
It's the flow and the ease that comes after the flood.
It's the depth, not the surface."

Jo Gifford, *Wild Currents*

There's a lovely meme going around at the moment on social media, all about choosing a plant in your home and calling it your name so that you can tend to it.

It becomes your focus to make sure this plant has water, that it has adequate light, that the dead leaves are pruned off, so that it can grow, and to keep coming back to be sure that it's thriving.

The idea being, of course, that once you set the habit of looking after this little plant and talking to it, nurturing it as you would yourself, that it then translates into your own life.

There's something really lovely about that image, I think. To see something visible outside of yourself that can really speak to how you nurture and look after yourself.

It's like a visual reminder every day of your self-care. A reminder to be kind to yourself, to make sure that you have that water, the air, the light and whatever those essential elements translate into in your daily life.

The same of course is true of the CLEAR Method and your environment, wherever that is, and however you live.

When we look around our environment and see clutter, layers of dirt, or corners that are forgotten, it's like a roadmap to the areas in our lives and in our energy fields that we are being called to gently look into.

There is no shame. There are no hard and fast rules during this stuff.

As you have hopefully discovered throughout this book, doing things little and often helps to reset habits. Very quickly by making tiny, tiny changes. Often the tipping point occurs before you know it, and you find yourself wanting to Clear, wanting to Receive wanting to Let Go, wanting to Activate and Energise. Once we turn that spiral back upwards, it really doesn't take very long, and results happen faster than you can imagine.

I like to think of it as a squeegee when you come out from the shower.

It's a tiny, little step that you build into your day, every day, just to wash away those water drops before they stain on the glass.

That's all the CLEAR Method is.

We're keeping your shower glass clear so that we can see.

We're helping you see in every way – with emotional clarity, physical space, and in your own journey to the 'clair,' the clear of knowing.

And, just like that habit happens after your daily shower, you will start to create habits that work for you, that Energise you, and that help you to thrive.

Clairvoyance, clairaudience, or clairsentience, might appear for you quickly.

It might be days, weeks, months, or even years.

But you will feel the CLEAR Method's effects in the time that's right for you, and they might appear in so many ways.

If cleaning has ever felt overwhelming and exhausting, that's often to do with all the stories around it that we may or may not have accumulated in our lives. Cleaning can feel insurmountable, that there is so much to do.

That's because we don't need to approach it all at once.

Go in tiny steps.

Let go of shame.

Clear the way – you de-mist the glass – do it as you go.

I'm so happy that you have embarked on your CLEAR Method adventure with me.

I just know that together you and the CLEAR Method will be shining a light on so many areas of your life.

I am sure that you will come back to pieces of this book when you need to – even if it's a sentence, even if it's just a word, over and over again.

Just remember, go at your own pace!

Love, Carolyn

X

CLEAR With Me

If you like what you have read so far, there are several ways you can CLEAR with me.

The CLEAR Circle

I am opening a CLEAR Circle Facebook Group – where I'll be dropping in to share tips and tricks on how to manage your spaces. If you would love to be a part of this circle – it is free to join and the link is https://www.facebook.com/groups/theclearcircle/

CLEAR Guidance Sessions

These come as a three session journey. Normally, a block or stuckness will nudge you in my direction. We will work through your block together, to help you become unstuck and allow the energy to flow wherever it needs to. These sessions are ideal if you want to declutter the chaos, and bring a little sparkle back into your life.

To enquire about these sessions please contact me on carolyn@carolyncreel.com and I'll see you right.

CLEAR Method Updates

I'm having loads of fun creating content for you at the moment, so you can catch me on Instagram @carolynspiritual

And on my website there will be a few offerings available for you to access straight away, and you can find me at www.carolyncreel.com

I look forward to connecting with you soon.

With Gratitude

Thank you Dear Reader for journeying with me. I truly hope that you have received the gift of Clarity, and have navigated the chaos that is life.

This book is for Chloe, my warrior princess, for proving that strength, trust and love will always get you where you need to be. You are everything to me. I love you.

To Jess, thank you for joining me on this journey, your enthusiasm is a joy to see, I am so proud of you !

To Adam, thank you for supporting me and allowing me the freedom to go and create this wonderful life.

To Anne and Fiona, your loyalty, willingness to listen and support is a joy to behold.

To my Family, those of you that are still here and those that are now in Spirit, I love you and I am so very grateful for all the lessons.

To Sarah, thank you for holding space and encouraging me when I doubted myself, and for creating your magic. This certainly would not have happened without you and your support.

To Jo, thank you for your magical words and cheerleading. You are the embodiment of joyful.

To Nicola and the team at the Unbound Press.

It's been a truly transformational experience.